*And It
Came to Pass
– Not to Stay*

Books by R. BUCKMINSTER FULLER

Nine Chains to the Moon

Untitled Epic Poem on the History of Industrialization

Ideas and Integrities

No More Secondhand God

Education Automation

Utopia or Oblivion

Operating Manual for Spaceship Earth

Intuition

Earth, Inc.

Synergetics: Explorations in the Geometry of Thinking

# AND IT
# CAME TO PASS
# -NOT TO STAY

## R. Buckminster Fuller

*Macmillan Publishing Co., Inc.*

NEW YORK

*Collier Macmillan Publishers*

LONDON

Macmillan Publishing Co., Inc.
866 Third Avenue, New York, N.Y. 10022
Collier Macmillan Canada, Ltd.

---

Library of Congress Cataloging in Publication Data

Fuller, Richard Buckminster, 1895–
    And it came to pass—not to stay.

    I.  Title.
PS3511.U661718      811'.5'4      76-18882
ISBN-0-02-541810-6

---

First Printing 1976

Printed in the United States of America

# Contents

# How Little I Know

"TELL ME
in five thousand
Written words"—
(Equivalent, at my oral rate,
To three-quarters of an hour's discourse)
"What you have learned—
In your lifetime,"
Said Norman Cousins.
"That ought to be easy," said I.

Three weeks have gone by—

I recall that
Thirty-eight years ago
I invented a routine
Somewhat similar to
Muscle development
Accomplished through
A day-by-day lifting
Of progressively heavier weights.

But my new
Intellectual routine
Dealt with the weightless process
Of human thought development
Which subject is
Known to the scholars
As *epistemology*.

And I have learned
That such words as Epistemology
Stop most of humanity
From pursuing
Such important considerations
As the development
Of the thought processes.

So my new discipline
Was invented for dealing
Even with the ephemeral
Which word means
*Conceptual but weightless—*
As is for instance
The *concept* of *circularity.*

My new strategy required
That on successive days
I ask myself
A progressively larger
And more inclusive question
Which must be answered
Only in the terms of
Experience.

Hearsaids, beliefs, axioms,
Superstitions, guesses, opinions
Were and are
All excluded
As answer resources
For playing my particular
Intellectual development game.

However, when lacking
Any possible experience clues
I saw that it was ineffectual
To attempt to answer

Such questions as for instance
"Why I?"
Or
"Why ...
Anything?"

And because it was my experience
That some individuals
Proved as persistently faithful
In reporting their experiences to me
As were my own senses
The rules of my game permitted
My inclusion of such individuals'
Directly reported experiences
In my inventory of experiences
For use in my progressively
Great and greater
Self-questioned answering.

In playing that game
I soon came
To what I assumed to be both
The largest askable and
The largest answerable
Question:
"What do you mean,"
I asked myself,
"By the word
Universe?
If you can't answer
In terms of
Direct experience
*You must desist*
*From the further use*
*Of the word UNIVERSE*
*For, to you*
*It will have become*
*Meaningless!"*

The 20th century physicists,
In defining physical Universe
As consisting only of energy,
Deliberately excluded metaphysical Universe—
Because the metaphysical
Consists only of imponderables,
Whereas the physical scientists
Deal only with ponderables—
Wherefore their physical Universe
Excluded for instance
All our thoughts—
Because thoughts are weightless—

But thoughts are experiences—
Wherefore I saw
That to be adequate
To the intuitively formulated
And experience-founded controls
Of my ever bigger
Question and answer routine,
My answering definition
Of UNIVERSE
Must be one which
*Embraced the combined*
*Metaphysical and physical*
*Components of UNIVERSE.*

Thus my self-formulating answer emerged,
And has persisted unshattered
By any subsequent challenges
From myself or others
As:
"By Universe I mean:
The aggregate of all humanity's
Consciously apprehended
And communicated
(To self or others)
*Experiences.*"

And later I discovered that
Eddington had said *"Science* is:
The conscientious attempt
To set in order
The facts of *Experience.*"

And I also discovered
That Ernst Mach—
The great Viennese physicist,
Whose name is used
to designate flight velocity
In *speed of sound* increments,
Known as Mach numbers—
Said:
"*Physics* is:
*Experience*
Arranged in
*Most economical order.*"

So I realized that
Both Eddington and Mach
Were seeking to put in *order*
The same "raw materials"—
*I.e. Experiences—*
With which to identify
Their special subsystems
Of UNIVERSE.

Wherefore I realized that
All the words in all dictionaries
Are the consequent tools
Of all men's conscious
And conscientious attempts
To communicate
All their experiences—
Which is of course
To communicate
Universe.

There are forty-three thousand current words
In the Concise Oxford Dictionary.
We don't know who invented them!
What an enormous, anonymous inheritance!
Shakespeare used ten thousand of them
With which to formulate
His complete "works."
It would take many more volumes
Than Shakespeare's to employ
The forty-three thousand—
Logically and cogently.

In a five thousand word article
I would probably have use for
Only one thousand.
Are forty-two thousand
Of these words
Superficial and extraneous
In reporting on
*What I have learned?*
I have learned that
You would think so
If you ever saw a magazine's
Space rewrite editor
At work on my work!

"What's stopping you?" said Norman.
"I'm not stopping—
I've never started.
I can't find the self starter
Or, more truthfully,
The self starter can't find me
Oh—there it goes"

Womb days—
Womb days—
Dear old tummy tomb days—

I can't consciously recall
Those busy elementary assembly days
But post-graduate activity in
Experimental biology
By me and you (one and two)
Which surprisingly produced
Wee thee (we three)
And more (four)
Suggest to us
That our subconscious reflexing
Can never forget
The satisfactory routines of our 273
Undergraduate days.
Probably no billionaire
Out here in the air
"Ever had it so good."

It is understood
That if you know that I know
How to say it "correctly"
(The exact meaning of which
I have not yet learned)
Then I am entitled to say it
All incorrectly
Which once in a rare while
Will make you laugh.
And I love you so much
Whenever you laugh.
But I haven't learned yet
What love may be
But I love to love
And love being loved
And that is a whole lot
Of unlearnedness.

I haven't learned yet
What laughter is

But a mother told me
How surprised was she
When an undergraduate first
Belly laughed in her
Alma mater
Dormitory.

I haven't learned
How or why
Universe contrived to implode
And intellectually code
The myriadly unique
Chromosomically orchestrated
DNA–RNA,
Quadripartite moleculed,
Binary paired,
Helically extended
And unzippingly dichotomied
Regenerative symphonic
Jazz, as
A one and two,
Three and four
Me – – – You,
Thee – – – they
And more
Thine and mine,
Sweet citizen.

 \* \* \* \* \* \* \* \*

THYMINE–CYTOSINE
GUANINE–ADENINE

 \* \* \* \* \* \* \* \*

That tetracouplet
Won the Nobel prize

The Wilkins, Crick and Watson Waltz

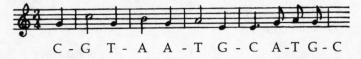

C - G  T - A  A - T  G - C  A-T-G - C

And that GC–TA jazz
All synced into
The nonsimultaneous aggregate
Of complex frequency integrated,
Multi-degrees-of-freedom permitted,
Individualized sequences,
Of experience evolutions,
Which we wave-modulatingly identify,
In the subconsciously formulated,
Tongue and lips shaped,
Omnidirectionally propagated,
Air wave patterning—
Sound
WORLD
—Whirled into the world
Of positive and negative
Of—

| MALE | and | FEMALE |
|---|---|---|
| Singular | and | Plural |
| Discontinuous | and | Continuous (has ovaries) |
| Compression | and | Tension |
| Hunter | and | Consolidator |
| Differentiator | and | Integrator |

| I | | O |
|---|---|---|
| I n | and | O u t |
| l I v e | and | l O v e |
| e v I l | and | e v O l |
| e v I l u t i o n | and | e v O l u t i o n |
| d e v I l | and | l O v e d |

The Devil lived
But never loved
Which is lonely—
L — one — only
As are all
Self I-s-O-lations

So let's withdraw
From exclusivity,
Into world music
Where—
As yet dancing to
The DNA waltz—
I am now seventy years, or
Approximately 600,000 hours old.
I have slept away 200,000 of those hours.

While another 200,000—
Which is half of
My 400,000 awake hours—
Have gone into routine work which has been
Prescribed, imposed or induced by other men—
Such as being "educated," earning a living,
Paying taxes, obtaining licenses,
Answering telephones and questionnaires.
And another 100,000—
Half of the remaining 200,000 awake hours—

Have gone also into routine work
But this time prescribed
In the by-laws of membership
In the nonsimultaneous invention, Universe—
As one of its impressively independent,
Variable functions—
A *human* member.

Each such member is
A metabolically regenerative
Ninety-nine percent automated,
Individually unique,
Abstract, pattern integrity system,
Whose input-output energy involvement
And control capability
Must continually expand, extend, relay, rebuild
And maintain, as "operative,"
An interior-exterior, bipartite tool complex
Beginning with an integrally centralized organic set

Which is subsequently extended into
An extracorporeally decentralized organic set.

Both of which interior and exterior sets consist of
Progressively interchangeable and intertransformable
Chemical, hydraulic, pneumatic,
Electromagnetic, thermodynamic,
Molecular and anatomical,
Structural patterning processes.

All of which complex
Regenerative processes
Are compounded as a unitary,
Invisibly minute,
Abstract pattern marriage operation,
Inaugurating a new individual life
Which like a telephone message
Has some of the thoughts of both parties
Yet weighs nothing in itself
But makes its compounded
Pattern self known
By a complex pattern of orderly and local
Physical environment displacements,
Which—as the circular wave
Emanating in any liquid
Such as water, milk or kerosene,
From the impact of an object
Dropped in the liquid—
Grows or expands regeneratively.

But as with the circularly expanding
Weightless wave emanation
There occurs also at outset
A momentary displacement exchange
As a centralized splash-back
Dissipated against gravity
To balance the local accounts.

And thus there is propagated
An abstract and weightless

Horizontally flowing
Wave impulse pattern integrity
Which though visibly apprehended
By its succession of local displacements
Does not consist of a horizontally moving
And ever increasing aggregate
Of water molecules.

There is another experiment
Which discloses the pattern integrity
Which can be demonstrated
By taking three different
Pieces of rope of equal diameter
One of manila
One of nylon
One of cotton
And making a beautiful running splice
Of one end of the manila rope
Into the end of the nylon rope
And the other end of the manila rope
Into the end of the cotton rope.

Next we make a simple back loop knot
In the end of the cotton rope
And slide it along the cotton rope
Until it slides along over the splice
Into the manila rope and along the manila
Until it slides past the splice
Onto the nylon
And makes it clear
That the knot is neither
Cotton, manila, nor nylon
But a pattern integrity
Made visible to us
By its temporary local displacement
Of the electromagnetic frequencies
Visible to us as colors
Within the frequency range
Tunable by our human optic system.

Neither water nor rope
"Went" anywhere
Only the weightless pattern integrity
Moved from here to there.

So too does the complex wave package
Of *human being* pattern integrity
Begin to compound and
Expand regeneratively
The local environment's chemical association
And disassociation events;
Continually shunting more
And more chemical event patterns
Into its local disturbance—
Like a tornado gaining twist,
Power and *visible presence* on Earth
By inhibiting ever
Greater quantities of
Locally available dust, fibers,
Water droplets and larger objects—
Until the new human being
Nine months later emerges
From its mother's womb
As a seven-pound, placid,
Pink tornado.

And this tomato-tinted tornado—me—
Swollen 24-fold to approximately 160 pounds—
Each day takes in and compoundingly processes
Approximately three pounds of foods,
Six pounds of water and
Sixty-four pounds of air—
From which it extracts six pounds of oxygen:—
Amounting at my seventy years
To a cumulative total
Of approximately 1,000 tons—
The weight of one United States Navy's
World War Two destroyer,
Or 300,000-fold my arrival weight.

But the thousand tons
Is in effect the weight
Of a seventy years long
Thirty-six inch girthed "rope"
Twisted of imaginary strands
Of food, water and air molecules
Drawn randomly from all around Earth,
And twisted temporarily together.

Into the molecular rope
A complex slip knot has been "tied"
Which complex knot
Is both internally and externally
In the exact pattern
Of the complex, pattern integrity:
Me—
Which has been slipped
Along the rope
By time.

And as the knot passed,
The rope behind it
Disintegrated and
Its atoms dispersed
And deployed into
Other biosphere function patternings.

Concurrently with "slipping" of corporeal "me"
The extracorporeally decentralized
Originally integral functions of "me"
Are externalized into a complex of tools
Averaging ten tons of steel,
Twenty-nine tons of concrete
Plus one mixed ton
Of all the other metals
Per each industrialized man.

And man's tool extensions
Process Universe energies,
Occurring only externally to man, and

Provide each 1965
North American type industrialized human
With two-hundred, 24-hour-serving, energy slaves;
Each slave being capable
Of doing as much physical work as
A human can do;
But at a ten millionfold
Finer degree of precision;
While working tirelessly
Under conditions of heat
And cold which would destroy man.

All of this combined internal and external
Metabolically regenerative man package
Arrives without any instruction manual
Covering either its own operation
Or that of nonsimultaneous Universe
Within which man must function
As an independent variable.
But the human package
Of integral and deployed tooling
Has fortunately
The built-in subconscious capability
Of self-discovery which in turn
Has discovered its conscious ability
To discover experimentally and progressively
The ability to formulate concepts and words
And thereby to relay to other contemporaries,
And to subsequent generations of man,
The apprehended data and
Comprehended principles
Apparently governing
Some of the Operations
Of Universe
Including man.

Of my remaining 100,000 hours
60,000 have been used
In getting from here to there;

And that has left me
A bonus of 40,000 hours
Or 6⅔ percent of my life's total hours
To invest at compound interest
In whatever way the
"Conscious" I
Wishes.

It is hard therefore to explain
Why conscious I
Should have behaved so perversely
As to have concentrated on producing
Explosives equivalent in destructive capability
To fourteen tons of TNT
Per each and every human on Earth.

And how perverse I have been
Is only to be comprehended
When it is realized
That the 14 tons per capita
Of self-annihilating explosives
Represents an energy harvest
Which if properly cultivated
Could have been made to support
At high standard of living
All human life on Earth
For all the rest
Of this century
While thus providing the opportunity
To invest the gained time
In providing for all
Human generations to come.

I'm not inclined to use
The word "Creativity"
In respect to human beings;
What is usually spoken of as creativity
Is really a unique and unprecedented

Human employment of *principles*
Which exist *a priori* in the Universe.

I think man is a very extra-ordinary
Part of the Universe
For he demonstrates unique capability
In the discovery and intellectual identification
Of the operative principles of Universe
—Which though unconsciously employed
Have not been hitherto differentiated,
Isolated out and understood
As being principles,
By other biological species.

Rejecting the word "creativity"
For use by any other than
The great intellectual integrity
Progressively disclosed as conceiving
Both comprehensively and anticipatorily
The complex interpatternings
Of reciprocal and transformative freedoms
In pure principle
Which apparently govern Universe
And constitute the verb god,
I go along with the 5,000-year-old
Philosophy of the Bhagavad-Gita
Which says "Action is the product
Of the qualities inherent in nature.
It is only the ignorant man,
Who, misled by personal egotism,
Says 'I am the doer.' "
I am most impressed
With the earliest recorded philosophic statements
By unknown individuals of India and China.
Through millenniums the philosophies
Have become progressively
Compromised and complicated.

I am an explorer, however,
Of the generalized design science principles
Which seemingly differentiate
Man from animal
And *mind* from *brain*.
The word "generalization"
As used in the *literary* sense,
Means "a very broad statement."
It suggests covering too much territory
—Too thinly to be sound.
The literary men say
"This is too general."

In the mathematical sense,
The meaning of generalization
Is quite different.
The mathematician or the physicist
Looks for principles which are
Persistently operative in nature,
Which will hold true in every special case.
If you can find principles
That hold true in every case,
Then you have discovered
What the scientist calls
A *generalized principle*.
The conscious detection of
Generalized principles which hold true
Under all conditions
And their abstraction from any and all
Special case experiences of the principles
—Is probably unique to humans.

By abstraction, I mean an idealized,
"Empty set" statement
Such as, for instance, one of my own!
—"Tension and compression are only coexistent"
—E.g., when you tense a rope

Its girth contracts—ergo compresses.
When you compress a sphere's polar axis,
Its equatorial girth expands and tenses,
It is inconceivable that a dog
Tugging at its leash at one time
And, compressing its teeth
On a bone at another time,
Should formulate consciously
The generalized
"Only coexistence of tension and compression,"
Though the dog is subconsciously coordinate
In tension-compression tactics.

To generalize further than
"Tension and compression are only coexistent,"
We may say that "plus and minus
Only coexist"
And generalize even further
By saying "Functions only coexist."
Then there is an even more powerful
And intellectually more exalted stage
Of generalization of principles
And that is the generalization
Of a complex of generalizations
—Such as—unity is plural and at minimum two
—Which combines the generalized law
Of the coexistence only of functions
With the theory of number.
In turn we discover the generalizations
Governing the associative powers
Of the nucleus and of the weak interactions
For the unity is two
Of the congruent, convex and concave spheres
As evidenceable in the generalized laws
Disclosed conceptually, arithmetically, and geometricall
In synergetics.

I am certain that what we speak of
As human morality

Is a form of tentative generalization
Of principles underlying
Special case experiences of human potentials,
Behaviors, actions, reactions and resultants.
Man has also the unique ability
To *employ* generalized principles
—Once recognized—
In a consciously selective variety
Of special case interrelationships.
The whole regenerative process
Of intellectual discovery
And specialized use of generalized principles
Is known as teleology.

Teleology embraces
The theory of communication,
Though as yet having special case limitations.
It is a hypothetical
Approach to pure, abstract generalization
To say that *teleology*
*Is only intuitively initiated by humans.*

Intuition alerts brain
To first apprehend
And then recognize
Each special case experience
Within some minimum number
Of special case recognitions.
Intuition alerts mind
To comprehend, and
Formulate conceptually
The abstract generalization
Of a principle recognized
As operative in all the special cases.
Intuition alerts brain to
The objectively employable generalized principle
In hitherto unexperienced special case
Circumstances inexplicably remote
From the earlier set of

Special case experiences within which
The generalized principles were first experienced
Before their generalization
Occurred in the mind.

Teleology—as part
Of communications theory
Relates to the pursuit of truth.
As entropy and antientropy.
It may be that
Communications theory
May be mathematically equated
With electrical
Transmission theory
Whereby the higher
The meaning or voltage
The more efficient
And longer distance
Communication attainable.

Based on experiments
with any *and* all systems,
The second law of thermodynamics
Predicts the inexorable energy loss
Known as ENTROPY.

Because the escaping energy
Does so diffusely,
In all directions,
Entropy is also known
Mathematically
As "The Law of Increase
Of the Random Element."

Before it had been discovered
By rigorous experimentation
That light has a *velocity*
It was erroneously assumed
To be "self-evident"

That light was instantaneous—
That all stars in the sky
Were "right there now"
In exact geometrical pattern,
Being seen instantaneously
And simultaneously
By all who looked their way.

But since Michelson's measurement
Of light's speed
We have learned that
The light from the Sun,
Our nearest star,
Takes eight minutes
To reach us here on Earth.
From our next nearest star
Light takes two years
To reach our planet Earth.
And other stars
Are so far away
Their light takes millions
Of years and more
To reach us.

Assuming instant-Universe
Classical Newtonian science
Also assumed that Universe
Must be an instant system—
A simultaneous unit machine,
In which every part
Must be affecting
Every other part,
In varying degrees
But in simultaneous unity.
They assumed also that the
Unit and simultaneous universe
Must of course obey
The great second law
Of thermodynamics

Whose, inexorable,
Entropic energy loss
Required self-dissipation
And ultimately utter
Self-annihilation
Of universe.
"Running down" they called it
Wherever "down" may be.

Though light's speed
Of seven hundred million miles per hour
Is *fast*
It isn't anywhere nearly as fast
As "instant"—
Which means reaching anywhere
"In no time at all."

Ergo, the Einsteinians
Instituted experiments
To ascertain the behavioral characteristics
Of a physical universe comprised
Of only partially overlapping,
Progressively intertransforming,
Nonsimultaneous, energy events.

The Einsteinian Era scientists' experiments
Showed that entropic energies
Accomplished their disassociations *here*
Only through associations *there*—
That is by regrouping elsewhere.
Thus early 20th-century scientists
Found the intertransformative
Energy quanta transactions,
To be eventually,
But not always immediately,
One hundred percent accountable.

As a consequence of
The Einsteinians' experiments

The eighteenth and nineteenth centuries'
Concept of a continually
Self-dissipating universe
Had to be abandoned
And in its place was established
The, experimentally required,
Law of Conservation of Energy
Which states that energy
May be neither created nor lost;
Ergo the energetic Universe
Is the minimum,
But nonsimultaneously realized,
Energy exchanging system,
Which is to say
That physical Universe,
As experimentally demonstrated
Is the minimum and only
Perpetual motion process,
Which as an aggregate of finite,
Dissimilar and nonsimultaneous
Energy events
Is in itself
Sum totally finite.

All the foregoing
Dissipates the foundations
Of the Newtonian world's
Cosmogony and economics
Which assumed
That a "running down world"
Suggested the prudence
Of saving, conserving and hoarding;
And that those who spent
Were fools who would perish
As resources dwindled.

Though entropically irreversible
Every action
Has its reaction and resultant,

And every nuclear component
Has its positive or negative
Behavioral opposite
Which is however
Not its mirror image.

And the irreversible situations
Give an evolutionary direction
To otherwise stalemated
Conditions of physical Universe.

For instance it is discovered
That wealth, whatever else it may be,
Cannot alter an iota of yesterday
And can alter only
The present and forward
Metabolic regeneration
Conditions of humanity.

Song of the Dead
And the Quick—
Newton was a noun
And Einstein is a verb.
Einstein's norm makes Newton's norm
INSTANT UNIVERSE,
Absurd.
"A body persists
In a state of rest
Or—
Except as affected—"
Thus grave stones are erected!

Nonsimultaneous, physical Universe
Is Energy; and
"Energy equals mass
Times the second power
Of the speed of light."
No exceptions!
Fission verified Einstein's hypothesis—

Change is normal
Thank you Albert!

Irreversible verse.
Einstein's intellect
Defined *energy* as $E = Mc^2$
*Energy* cannot define *intellect*.
Intellect the *metaphysical*
Is comprehensive to
Energy the *physical*.
While Universe is *finite*
Energy is *definite*
Because definable
Energy is XY.
Intellect is 0.
The wealth of Earthians
Is irreversible.
Wealth cannot alter yesterday's experience.
It can only alter today's and tomorrow's experiences.
It can buy
Forward time in which intellect
May scientifically explore for
The orderly interrelationships
Disclosed in yesterday's experiences
Which can be employed by intellect
To forecast
Anticipatory and orderly rearrangements of tomorrow
By technological transformations
Of the physical energy environments,
Events and circumstances.

Wealth is the organized and operative
Tools and energy capability
To sustain man's forward metabolic regeneration;
To physically protect him;
To increase his knowledge
And degrees of freedom
While decreasing his interfrustrations.
Solo wealth is to commonwealth

As X is to $X^4$.
Wealth is: *Energy compounded*
*With intellect's know-how.*

Every time man uses his *know-how*
His experience increases
And his intellectual advantage
Automatically increases.
Because of its *conservation*
Energy cannot decrease.
Know-how can only increase.
It is therefore scientifically clear
That:—wealth which combines
Energy and intellect
Can *only increase,* and that wealth can
Increase *only with use*
And that wealth increases
As fast as it is used.
The faster—the more!

Wealth is accountable as
The inanimate energies shunted
Onto the ends of industrial levers
Whose physical capability is
Stateable in forward, automated,
Man days of travel miles
With first class comprehensive services
Including food, lodging, clothing,
Amusements, communication, information
And medical services
Based on the average physical experiences
Of a top civil service rating's
World travel involvements.

Has man a function
In Universe?

In dynamical balance
With the inside-outing,
*Expanding universe*

Of radiant stars,
Man witnesses
Radiantly dormant Earth as
A collecting or outside-inning,
*Contracting phase*, of Universe.
Earth receives and stores,
A continually increasing inventory
Of sun and star emanating radiation
In its lethal-energy-concentrates
Sifting, sorting and accumulating
Spherical Van Allen belts.

In addition to the Van Allen belts
The succession of Earth's concentric
Spherical mantles, e.g.,
The ionosphere, troposphere *et al.*,
Constitute an extraordinary series
Of discrete filters for
The random-to-orderly sorting,
Shunting, partially accumulating
And final inwardly forwarding
Of the benign radiation residues
To the biosphere stage
Of Earth's continual and orderly
Processing of its discrete share
Of the expanding-Universe-propagated
Energy income receipts.
Earth also receives daily
Additional thousands of tons
Of expanding-Universe-dispatched
Stardust.

This concentration around Earth's surface
Of the Universe-deposited dust
Apparently consists of 91 of the
92 regeneratively patterning
Chemical elements
In approximately the same systematic order
Of relative abundance of those elements

As the relative abundance
Of those same elements
As they are found to occur
In the thus far inventoried
Reaches of Universe.
The biological life on earth
Is inherently antientropic
For it negotiates the chemical sorting
Out of the Earth's crust's
Chemical element inventory
And rearranges the atoms
In elegantly ordered
Molecular compound patternings.
Of all the biological antientropics,
I.e., random-to-orderly arrangers,
Man's intellect is by much
The most active, exquisite and effective agent
Thus far in evidence in Universe.
Through intellect, man constantly succeeds
In inventing technological means
Of doing ever more orderly
I.e., more efficient,
"Better sorted-out,"
Local Universe, energy tasks
With ever less units of investments
Of the (what may be *only apparently*),
"*Randomly*" *occurring*
Resources of energy,
As atomic matter,
Or *energy* as *channeled electromagnetics.*

To guarantee
All of life's
Antientropic functioning,
Intellectual integrity Universe
Which has designedly arranged the great game
Has also arranged that mankind,
Like all the other living species,

Has its ultra-shortsighted,
Built-in, "desire" drives,
Its romantic conception ambitions
And protectively colored self deceits,
As well as its longer distance "needs,"
All of which cause each species
To pursue its particular "honey"
With its particular rose-colored glasses,
As does the bumblebee
Which at the same time
Inadvertently and unconsciously performs
Myriads of other tasks,
Designed with fabulous
Scientific capability by nature,
Which inadvertent interco-ordinate tasks
Unknown to the separate creature species
Are all essential to realization
Of the regenerative continuance
Of the much larger
Survival support conditions
For the generalized
Ecological system of "all life."

It is part of
The comprehensively anticipating,
Design science of life
That the bumblebee's self-unviewed,
Unwitting, bumbling tail
Bumps into and knocks off male pollen,
Which it later
And again inadvertently,
Knocks off upon the female botanical organs,
Thus unconsciously participating in
A vastly complex ecological interaction
Of the many energy processing
Bio-chemical "gears"
Of the total life system
Dynamically constituted by
All the living species.

The myriad inadvertencies
Of all the living species
Have sum totally provided
A metabolically sustaining
And regenerative topsoil process
Which—it is realized now,
But only by
Our retrospectively gained knowledge—
Has kept man
Regeneratively alive on Earth
For at least two million years,
While ever improving
His physical survival advantages
And increasing his longevity.

This vast "game playing" of life
Has also indirectly occasioned
Not only the regenerative multiplication
Of human beings,
But also a progressively increasing
Percentage who survive in conditions
Of ever improving
Physical advantage.

I think man is very properly concerned
About that which he does not understand.
I don't think that it is the machine per se
That bothers man;
It is just not understanding
Anything
That disturbs him.
When an accident bares
Portions of human organs
Familiar only to doctors,
Those organs look foreign
And frightening to people.
Stick your tongue way out
Before a mirror.
It is a strange looking device.

If existing originally and
Transcendentally as psyches only,
Individuals had to choose,
And assemble their own sets
Of organic parts,
Having been assured of mortal incarnation
And of mortal "honey chasing" experiences
But only after successful selection
And completion of the assembly—
And were endowed—as psyches—
Only with an aesthetic
Sense of selectivity,
Being devoid of any understanding
Of either the separate or integrated
Functions of those parts—
No humans would merger
Those co-operatively functioning parts
Into mortal beings
For no part of the "guts"
Would be chosen.
Nature had to skin over the regenerative
Chemistry and physics controls,
With an aesthetically intriguing,
Pseudo-static, sculptural baby doll unity
In order to trick the immortal psyches
Into the problem-beset,
Temporary occupation
Of such humid process regenerative machines
As those of the humans.

I have learned
That man knows little
And thinks he knows a lot.
When any man can tell us
Just how and why he is handling and disposing
The energies of his breakfast;
How he breaks down his chemical energy and
To which glands he is routing

The diversified energies of his ham and eggs;
Or when any man can tell us
That he is deliberately
Pushing each of his million
Head hairs
Out through his scalp
At specifically preferred rates
And in specifically controlled shapes
For specific purposes,
We may say that this man
Knows a little,
But I don't know of any man
Who can tell me
So little even as
Why we have hair.

I am the most unlearned man I know.
I don't know anyone
Who has learned
How little one knows
As have I.
But that does not belittle
The little I seem to know,
And I have confidence
In the importance of remembering
How little we know
And of the possible significance
Of the fact that we prosper,
And at some times even enjoy
Life in Universe
Despite the designed-in littleness
That we have to "get by with."

I like algebra

Positives more powerful than negatives

$$(+) \times (-) = (-) \quad \text{minus wins}$$
$$(+) \times (+) = (+) \quad \text{plus wins only by default}$$
$$(-) \times (-) = (+) \quad \text{plus wins}$$

The game is over—
Plus wins two to one.


What the astronomers rank as
The nearest "bright" star to Earth
Is "Rigel Kent"
Which is three hundred thousand times
Further away from Earth than is the Sun.
It is easy to see a man
One third of a mile away and
We were surprised when young
To see a man
At that distance
Swinging a sledge
To drive a post into the ground
And to realize
That the sound of his maul
Hitting the post top
Registered in our brain
As reported through the ears
Four seconds later
Than had the visual news
Which "long since" had told us
That he had once more
Hit the post.
Through physical experiments
Performed by our scientists
We have learned that
The highest known velocity
Among physical phenomena
Is the speed of light and all radiation
Relayingly scanned by nerve lines
To our brain's television conceptualizing
Through the optics of our eyes.


Because the speed of light
Is approximately 186,000 miles per second,
And the Moon is

About twice that distance
Away from Earth.
If we had a large mirror on the Moon,
And we flashed a powerful
Light toward the Moon
It would take four seconds
For the light to be reflected back
To our eyes.
That is, the light takes
Two seconds to get to the Moon
And two more seconds
To return to Earth.
And the overall four seconds lag
Of the visual report
Is the same time lag as that in
Our childhood realized lag
Of the *sound report*
Behind the *visual report*
Of the post-sledging event.
Because the light coming to Earth
From the Moon
Takes two seconds to make the trip,
And because the light
Coming to Earth from the Sun
Takes eight and one-half minutes,
And because the light
Coming to us from Rigel Kent
Takes four and one-half years,
We all see a live show
Taking place in the sky
Four and one-half
Years ago.

And as we gaze around
The starry heavens
We see right now
Live shows of "yesterdays"
Ranging from millions to sextillions of years ago,
As we look at the stars

We see all of history
Now alive.

It took only two million years and
Four and one-half billion human babies
To establish a human survival beachhead
Aboard the little
Eight-thousand-mile-diameter
Spherical Spaceship EARTH
Whereby life could successfully realize
Its highest known potential life span
Possibly to continue indefinitely
As one self-rejuvenation generation.
Few of the stars we look at,
Live-starring out there,
Are young enough
To witness
Those first human events
Taking place on Earth
Only two millions of years ago.

Since all the vital parts
Of human organisms
Have now become interchangeable,
And many of them
Have also become interchangeable
With inanimate mechanical parts,
And since human longevity
Is continually increasing
There is a good possibility
That humanity is developing
A continuous human
Who will persist in prime health
And youthful vigor

With the lessening of need
To replenish the population
With fresh baby starts,
The built-in drives to procreate

Will lessen and be manifest in a proclivity
Of females to camouflage as male
And males to camouflage as female
Thus suppressing the procreative urge
By superficial antipathetic illusions,
While permitting and promoting
Procreatively innocuous sex companionships.

Despite their billionfold numbers
Babies and very young children
Soon after their arrival on Earth
Have uttered and continue to utter
Spontaneous comments and questions—
Concerning life on Earth
And in Universe—
Which are so economical
And uniquely fresh
In viewpoint and formulation
As to be pure poetry
Apparently proving that
poetry is inexhaustible;
To which their sophisticated
And surprised off-guard adult audience
Cliché unpoetically
"Oh how cute."

In the year 1964
The one hundred largest
Industrial giant corporations,
Born and reared
In the United States of America
Invested four out of five
Of their new plant and equipment
Expansion dollars
In production and service facilities
In world lands outside the U.S.A.
This trending to World identity only
Of the industrial giants
Held true also not only with thousands

Of lesser magnitude
U.S.A. and European born
Limited liability industrial organizations
But also with the Communist countries'
Giant industrial organizations.
Wherefore world industrialization trends swiftly—
And altogether transcendentally
To man's conscious planning—
Into an unitarily co-ordinate
World giant
With built-in automated,
Research fed,
Computer analyzed and selected,
Evolutionary self-improving
And self-transforming
Through alternatingly regenerated
Competitive precessioning
Of all the variable functions
Of general systems theory.

TRUTH
I have learned that truth
Is an omnipresent, omnidirectional,
Evolutionary awareness,
One of whose myriadly multiplying facets
Discloses that there are no "absolutes"
—No "ends in themselves"—no "things"
—Only transitionally transformative verbing.

It seems possible to me
That god may be recognizable
In man's limited intellection
Only as the weightless passion drive
Which inspires our progressive searching
For the—momentarily only—
And only most-truthful-thus-far-possible—
Comprehension of all the interconnections
Of all experiences.

It seems then to me
That the nearer we come to understanding,
The nearer we come to the
Orderly omni-interrelationships
Of all the weightless complex
Of all generalized principles
Which seem to be disclosed to us
As so important
As to be tentatively identified as God.
For it is the integratable interrelationships
Of all the generalized laws
Which apparently govern
The great verb "Universe"
Of the vastly greater
—Because comprehensively anticipatory—
Verb *intellecting*
Which verb of optimum understanding
May be "God."

It seems that Truth
Is progressive approximation
In which the relative fraction
Of our spontaneously tolerated *residual error*
*Constantly diminishes.*

This is a typical
Antientropy proclivity of man
—Entropy being the law
Of *increase of the random element.*

Heisenberg's indeterminism,
In which the act of measuring
Always alters the measured,
Would seem entropic were it not
For the experimentally realized knowledge
That the successive alterations
Of the observed
Diminish

As both our tooling and instrumentation
Continually improve;
Ergo intellection's effect
Upon measurement and the measured
Is a gap closing,
And the pursuit of more truthful comprehension
Is successfully antientropic.

Before Heisenberg, T. S. Eliot said,
"Examination of history alters history"
And Ezra Pound,
And even earlier poets,
Reported their discoveries
That in one way or another
The act of thinking alters thought itself.

When we ask ourself
"What have we learned?"
We feel at first
That the answer is "nothing."

But as soon as we say so
We recall exceptions.
For instance we have learned
To test experimentally
The axioms given to us
As "educational" springboards, and
We have found
That most of the "springboards"
Do not spring
And some never existed.
As for instance
Points, holes,
Solids, surfaces,
Straight lines, planes,
"Instantaneous," "simultaneous,"
Things, nouns,
"Up," "down," "at rest"
The words "artificial" and "failure"
Are all meaningless.

For what they aver
Is experimentally "non-existent."
If nature permits a formulation
It is natural.
If nature's laws of behavior
Do not permit the formulation
The latter does not occur.
Whatever can be done
Is natural,
No matter how grotesque, boring,
Unfamiliar or unprecedented.
In the same way
Nature never "fails."
Nature complies with her own laws.
*Nature is the law.*
When man lacks understanding
Of nature's laws
And a man-contrived structure
Buckles unexpectedly,
It does not fail.
It only demonstrates that man
Did not understand
Nature's laws and behaviors.
Nothing failed.
Man's knowledge or estimating
Was inadequate.

Step to the blackboard.
Write out a number so lengthy
It has never been written before.
The pattern of numbers
Constitutes a new form.
The number is a doodle.
And I cannot accredit novel form
As creativity of man.
The number of relationships between items
Is always $\dfrac{N^2 - N}{2}$.

The relationships between four or more items
Are always greater in number
Than the number of items.
Ergo, there are always more chords than notes
And chords by themselves are not music.
It takes two to make a baby
But it takes God to make two.

God is twoing
God is threeing
God is multiplying
By dividing
The second law of thermodynamics—
Entropy—is also as we have learned
The law of increase of the Random Element
I.e., every system looses energy—but
Synergy means
Behavior of whole systems
Unpredicted by
The behavior of any separate part.

EN–ergy behaves entropically.
SYN—ergy behaves syntropically.
God is entropy
And God is syntropy,
God is synergy.
God is energy.
And God is always
A verb—
The verbing of
Integrity.

I assume that the *physical Universe is definite*
And the *metaphysical Universe is finite.*
What men have called infinite
I call finite
And what men called finite
I call definite—i.e., definitive.

By my philosophy
The finite, but imponderable
Metaphysical Universe
Embraces the definite,
Ponderable, physical Universe.
*Finite* is not unitarily conceptual.
*Definite* is unitarily conceptual.
I have mathematical proof
That the difference between the sums
Of all the angles around all the surface vertices
Of any conceptual, definitive physical system
And the finite but non-conceptual metaphysical universe
Is always 720 degrees
Or a difference of only one
*Definitive tetrahedron,*
Therefore, the combined
Physical and metaphysical Universe is finite.

You can't buy anything worthwhile
Like spontaneous *love* or *understanding*.
Though metaphysically finite
These are imponderables.

The absolute would be
Nontransformable, static and weighable.
Ergo, experimentally meaningless.
Infinity is only local
And occurs within definite systems,
As for instance
Following a great circle
Around a sphere
Which because of the fact
That lines—
Which occur experimentally
Only as energy vectors—
Cannot go through
The same point
At the same time—
Due to interference,

Which means also that lines
As curves
Cannot re-enter, or
"Join back into themselves,"
Therefore, the circling line
Can only wrap around
And over its earlier part—
As the knot-making
Sailor says it,
The circle when followed
Around and around
Results in a coil
Which is an endless scenario—
An asymmetric spiral,
Which may be followed experimentally
Only as long as intellect is interested.

Not being simultaneous
Universe cannot consist of one function.
Functions only coexist.
Universe while finite is not definable.
I can define many of its parts
But I cannot define simultaneously
The nonsimultaneously occurring
Aggregate of partially overlapping experiences
Whose total set of local scenario relationships
Constitutes the whole Universe
Though the latter as an aggregate of finites
Is finite.
All the words
In all the dictionaries, as noted before,
Represent all of humanity's attempts
To express the aggregate of experiences—Universe.
And while the dictionaries are finite
All the words
In all the dictionaries
Cannot be read simultaneously
And there is not one
Simultaneous sentence

Inherent and readable
In all the words.
In the same way
All the nonsimultaneous experiences
May not be conceived
And expressed as
A simultaneous system.
Ergo, there is no thinkable and logical
Simultaneous conception
Of nonsimultaneous Universe.

There is strong awareness
That we have been overproducing
The army of rigorously disciplined
Scientific, game playing, academic specialists
Who through hard work
And suppressed imagination
Earn their Ph.D.'s
And automatic contracts
With prime contractors
At fifteen thousand dollars
Per year—and more—
Only to have their specialized field
Become obsolete and by-passed in five years,
By severely altered techniques, instruments
And exploratory stratagems.
Despite their honor grades
They prove not to be
The Natural Philosophers
And scientist-artists, implied by their Ph.D.'s
But just deluxe quality
Technicians or mechanics.
And a myriad
Of emergency committees—
Multiplying swiftly
From one or two
Emergency Committees
Appointed by the President,
Have altogether discovered

That what the
Ph.D. scientists lack—
To adapt themselves to change
Has been officially pronounced to be
"Creativity,"
But to my thinking
They lack the unique capability of mind—
Which is the ability not only to generalize
And to integrate a complex
Of pure generalizations
But also to project teleologically—
With fundamental understanding—
In any special case direction.
Fundamental wisdom
Can readily identify any and all
Special case aspects within
The generalized whole
When listening
Sensitively to one's intuitions
By which alone
The generalized sub-subconscious integration
Of pattern cognition feedbacks
Are articulated.

Philip Morrison—Cornell's head
Of the department of nuclear physics—
Talks about what he calls
"Left-hand" and "right-hand" sciences.
Right-hand science deals in all the proven
Scientific formulas and experiments.
Left-hand science deals in
All of the as yet *unknown* or *unproven*—
That is: With all it is going to take
Intellectually, intuitively, speculatively, imaginatively
And even mystically
By inspired persistence
To open up the as yet unknown.
The great scientists were great
Because they were the ones

Who dealt successfully with the unknown.
All the "greats" were left-hand scientists.
Despite this historical patterning of the "greats"
We have government underwriting
Only the right-hand science,
Making it bigger and sharper,
Rather than *more inclusive* and *understanding!*—
For how could congress justify
Appropriations of billions for dreams?
So the billions went only
For the swiftly obsoleting
Bigger, faster and more incisive
Modifications of yesterday's certainties,
By Ph.D. specialists
Guaranteed by the great
Institutes of Technology
To which the congress
Allocated the training funds
As obviously "safe"
And exempt from political criticism;
Despite that scientific investigation
Had shown beyond doubt
That almost all of America's
Top performance scientists
Had been educated
In small, liberal arts colleges,
And that almost all
Of those top scientists
Attributed their success
To their good fortune
In having studied intimately
With a great inspiring teacher.
It would be considered
Political madness
To risk charges of corruption
Through voting government funds
To any individual
Especially to "great inspiring teachers"—
"Crackpot longhairs!"

So it goes—
To hell with the facts
When re-election
To political office is at stake.

Everything that constitutes science
Is unteachable.

And we recall that
Eddington said: "Science
Is the earnest attempt
Of *individual initiative*
To set in order
The facts of experience."
Scientific routines for specialized technicians
And scientific formulas for their reference
Alone are teachable. Initiative is unteachable.

Because we have been governmentally fostering
Only right-hand science and
Right-hand science to excess
The U.S.A. President's science advisor
Instituted last year (1965)
A new direction of search
For sources of so-called "creativity."
Financed by the National Academy of Sciences,
He asked New York University's art department
To bring together a representative group of
America's leading art educators and artists.
It was felt by the National Academy
That the art educators—
As those who dealt with
Most of the almost drop-outs
Who had been switched into art
As a "last resort"—
Were probably intimate
With the type of emerging youth
Who were allowed to remain
In a freer state of mind
—In the world of art—

Than would they have been
If disciplined rigorously
In sharp specialization by the sciences.
That meeting, I thought fascinating
For it disclosed the artists as being
Individuals who develop powerful self-protection
Of their innate intellectual
And conceptual capability inheritance.
They often protect their innate capabilities
Through intuitively triggered poker-faced silence
Which in the elementary or high schools
Is interpreted as non-cooperative, mental inferiority,
Often causing early termination
Of their formal education.
I think the consensus
Of the New York University meeting
Was that individuals
Of original conceptual brilliance
Were most frequently
Detected, protected, and made to grow
By equally sensitive art teachers.
"Great teachers."
Which agrees elegantly
With the statements
Of the proven scientists
Regarding their own experiences.
Congressional appropriations committees
Please take notice!

To comprehend the integral of art and science
As an irrepressible, intuitive creative urgency—
As an artist's need to articulate—
Kepes at Massachusetts Institute of Technology
Made a beautiful demonstration.

He took hundreds of 8″ × 10″
Black-and-white photographs
Of modern paintings and mixed them thoroughly
Like shuffled cards
With photographs taken by scientists

Through microscopes or telescopes
Of all manner of natural phenomena
Sound waves, chromosomes and such.
The only way you can classify
Photographs with nothing recognizable in them
Is by your own spontaneous
Pattern classifications.
Group the mealy, the blotchy, the striped,
The swirly, the polka-dotted, and their sub-combinations.
The pattern classified groups
Of photographs were displayed.
The artists' work and the scientists'
Were indistinguishable.
Checking the back-mounted data, it was found
That the artist had frequently conceived
The imagined pattern before
The scientist found it in nature.
Science began to take
A new view of artists.

Loving mothers
Prohibit here and promote there—
Often in ways irrelevant or frustrating
To brain-coordinated genetic evolution,
Often suppressing
A child's profound contribution
Trying to emerge.
We have to look on our society
As we look on the biological world in general
Recognizing, for instance,
The extraordinary contributions
Of the fungi, the manures, the worms, *et al.*—
In the chemical reprocessing—
And fertility up-grading of the earth.
We must learn to think
Of the functions of the trees' roots
As being of equal importance
To the leaves' functions.
We tend to applaud

Only the flower and the fruit
Just as we applaud only the football player
Who makes the touchdown
And not the linemen
Who opened the way.

What society applauds as "creative"
Is often isolated
Out of an extraordinary set
Of co-equal evolutionary events,
Most of which are invisible.
Evolutionary "touchdowns" are unpredictable—
Sometimes centuries apart.
Who knows which child is to make the next breakthrough?
In the next decade society
Is going to be preoccupied with the child
Because through the behavioral sciences
And electrical exploration of the brain
We find that given the right environment
And thoughtful answers to its questions
*The child has everything it needs educationally*
*Right from birth.*

We have thought erroneously of education
As the mature wisdom
And over-brimming knowledge of the grownups
Injected by the discipline pump
Into the otherwise "empty" child's head.
Sometimes parents say "don't"
Because they want to protect the child
From getting into trouble.
At other times when they fail to say "no"
The child gets into trouble.
The child, frustrated, stops exploring.
It is possible to design environments
Within which the child will be
Neither frustrated nor hurt
Yet free to self-educate, spontaneously and fully
Without trespassing on others.
I have learned to undertake

Reform of the environment
And not to try to reform man.
*If we design the environment properly*
It will permit both child and adult to develop safely
And to behave logically.

Order is achieved through—positive and negative—
Magnitude and frequency controlled alteration
Of the successive steering angles.
We move by zigzagging control
From one phase of physical Universe evolution to another.
The rudder concept of social law is most apt.
The late Norbert Wiener chose the word *cybernetics*
Derived from Greek roots of "rudder"
Because Wiener, Shannon and others in communication theory
Were exploring human behaviors
And their brain-controlled "feedback," etc.,
As a basis for the design of computers—
And it became evident
That the human brain only waveringly
Steers man through constant change.

No sharp cleavage is found
Which identifies the boundary between life and non-life,
Between the heretofore so-called "animate" and "inanimate."
Viruses,
The smallest organized structures
Exhibiting "life,"
May be classified either
As inanimate or animate—
As crystalline or "cellular" forms.
This is the level also at which
The DNA-RNA genetic code serves as
An angle and frequency designed
Structural pattern integrity.
Such pattern integrities
Are strictly accountable
Only as mathematical principles
Pattern integrities are found
At all levels of structural organization in Universe.

The DNA-RNA is a specialized case
Of the generalized principle of pattern integrity
Found throughout life and non-life.
All pattern integrity design
Is controlled entirely and only by
Angle and frequency modulation.
The biological corpus
Is not strictly "animate" at any point.
Given that the "ordering"
Of the corpus design
Is accomplished through such codings as DNA-RNA
Which are exclusively angle and frequency modulation.

Then we may go on to suggest
That "life," as we customarily define it
Could be effected at a distance.
Precession is the effect
Of one moving system
Upon another moving system.
Precession always produces
Angular changes of the movements
Of the effected bodies and
At angles other than 180 degrees,
That is, the results are never
Continuance in a straight line.
Ergo all bodies of universe
Are effecting the other bodies
In varying degrees
And all the intergravitational effects
Are precessionally angular modulations
And all the interradiation effects
Are frequency modulations.

The gravitational and radiation effects
Could modulate the DNA-RNA
Angle and frequency instructions
At astronomical remoteness—
Life could be "sent on."

Within the order of evolution as usually drawn

Life "occurred" as a series
Of fortuituous probabilities in the primeval sea.
It could have been sent or "radiated" there.
That is, the prime code
Or angle and frequency modulated signal
Could have been transmitted
From a remote stellar location.
It seems more likely
(In view of the continuous rediscovery of humans
As fully organized beings
At ever more remote historical periods)
That the inanimate structural pattern integrity,
Which we call human being,
Was a frequency modulated code message
Beamed at Earth from remote location.
Man as prime organizing
"Principle" construct pattern integrity
Was radiated here from the stars—
Not as primal cell, but as
A fully articulated high order being,
Possibly as the synergetic totality
Of all the gravitation
And radiation effects
Of all the stars
In our galaxy
And from all the adjacent galaxies
With some weak effects
And some strong effects
And from all time.
And pattern itself being weightless,
The life integrities are apparently
Inherently immortal.

You and I
Are essential functions
Of Universe
We are exquisite syntropy.

I'll be seeing you!
Forever.

# Complexion* 1976

*Webster's Third New International Dictionary,
meaning 2b: an individual complex of attitudes,
inclinations, or ways of thinking or feeling

Wᴴᴇɴ ɴᴏᴛɪɴɢ the cosmic myopia
Dominating the leaders
Of the variety of Earthian power-structures
At this particular celestial and terrestrial
Cosmic-history moment
We do not impute malevolence or wrongdoing
On the part of any
Individuals or groups.

What we *are doing* is:
Endeavoring to discover
The responsibly operative
Evolutionary check-and-balance mechanisms
Of Scenario Universe's nonsimultaneously occurring
And everywhere only partially overlapping variety
Of exquisitely discrete, local,
Conception-to-birth
Gestation and degestation rates,
Whose overlappingly interbraided strands
Of unique velocities, intensities and durations
Constitute the complex intersynchronizings
Of both the associative and disassociative
Energy event frequencies
—Those of the newborn, youthful growth accelerations
Integrated with the agings, slowings and dyings off.
On a strict
Universe resource accounting basis
The overall complex intersynchronizing
Manifests no loss in the physical inventory
And an ever-increasing metaphysical inventory
Of know-what, know-where and know-how/wealth.

The magnitude of MONEY WEALTH
Is manifest as the number
Of healthfully adequate and regenerative
Present and forward days of the minority's
Life support and accommodation for which
The lethally intercompetitive sovereign states,
Transnational corporations, cartels and capital anarchists
Have organized the world's
Physical and metaphysical resources to provide,
While also diverting a large amount
Of the evolution-realized increases
In scientific and technical capabilities
Exclusively into money-making for a few
Or into armed protection
Of their special individual advantaging.


REAL WEALTH is manifest
As the magnitude to which the effectiveness
Of realized MONEY WEALTH can be multiplied
By full intercooperative effort
Of all humanity
When using their world-around combined
Physical and metaphysical resources
As practically realizable
At any one moment
Of ever advancing engineering efficiency
Ever regeneratively reinvested
Exclusively and directly
Only in the support and freedoms accommodation
Of all human life.

Humanity is consistently acquiring
Ever greater performance effectiveness know-how
In providing life support
And in accommodating freedom of initiative
For ever more people
With ever less physical resource investments
For each per capita task accomplished.

The energy for regenerating
All biological life on Earth
Comes exclusively from the stars
And almost exclusively from the star Sun.
Humans and other mammals
Cannot convert Sun energy directly
Into metabolic life support.
Vegetation and algae constitute
The only known biological means
Of converting random celestial radiation receipts
Into support of terrestrial life.

In the photosynthetic chemical processes
Of converting random cosmic energy receipts
Into orderly hydrocarbon molecules
Which may be assimilated and proliferated
By all the biologicals
The vegetation also takes in
Certain of the atmospheric gases
While giving off other
Of its original gaseous elements set
Which process would soon convert
All the terrestrial atmosphere
Into the non-photosynthesis-enabling gases,
A condition which soon would frustrate
Further Earthian photosynthesis
Which in turn would terminate
Biological inhabitance of planet Earth.

To cope with this cosmic design problem
Human beings and the other mammals
Are designed to inhale and use growthfully
The vegetation emitted gases
While reconverting into and exhaling
Those chemical gases which are essential
To vegetation's continuance of photosynthesis.

The design integrity
Of eternally regenerative Universe
Involves a myriad of such

Locally regenerative intercomplementations,
Chemical and physical energy transactions
And intertransformation recyclings
Whereby in turn
Humanity's locally supportive potentials as
Metaphysical understandings of such phenomena
May emerge, evolve, and multiply on planet Earth
Potentially to evoke and sustain
The birth and experiential development of humanity's
Exclusively metaphysically conceived
Artifact and service-system inventions
Which again in turn may support
Humanity's brain-apprehended
Information inventorying
And human mind's further discovering
Of additional generalized principles
Existing as covarying relationships
Always consistently operative
Only within and between
The human brain's neuron sorted and stored
Exclusively special case information inventory.

All of the progressive ecological intersupporting
Was and is designed to sustain
The total cosmic regenerative system
Which includes not only all humanity
But also the terrestrial, ecological regenerative system
Which in turn includes
Not only the biological organisms
And all their geological and biospheric surroundings
But also the interaction
Of the planetary regenerative system
With the omnicelestial regenerative system
Of the macro-micro Universal Scenario.

The purely physical, cosmic regenerativity
Is maintained on Earth—
As cosmic, failsafe alternate recircuitry—

By intense, high-frequency information
(Electromagnetic frequencies)
Transmitted by the chemical elements of the star Sun,
And receivingly translated
By the Earth's landborn vegetation
And waterborn algae
Into photosynthetic sorting,
Reorganizing and combining
Of the planet Earth's
Local chemical element inventory
Of carbon, hydrogen, and other elements,
Some of which informational energies
Are redistributed to the biosphere,
While some re-enter directly
Into the integral metabolic
Multiplication and proliferation
Of all biological organisms
As the hydrocarbon molecules
Originally produced photosynthetically
By the vegetation.

For Earthborn vegetation
To function successfully
(A)
Structurally in storms
While exposing adequate leafage to the Sun,
It must send anchorage roots into the soil
And between the rocks
With which roots also
(B)
To osmotically draw water from the soil
Wherewith to watercool their leaf systems
To avoid dehydration
By the heats of vast radiation exposure
As well as
(C)
To employ the antigravitational
Exclusively one-way

Valving and pumping process of osmosis
To physically structure the vegetation
With a noncompressible hydraulic liquid substance
Contained within high tension crystalline cell sacks
Altogether capable of omni-equidistribution
Of the many eccentric,
Locally concentrated energy loadings and stressings
Omnidiverted to all the tensionally enclosing elements
While also
(D)
Vaporizing the water
Drawn outward from the ground
Through the trees' osmotic system
So that the vaporized water
May be transformed by the *sun*
Into windborn clouds
To be precipitated as rain
Upon other vegetation
Growing elsewhere around the planet.

Because the vegetation is rooted,
It cannot reach the other vegetation
To procreate
To solve this regenerative problem
Universe designed the vast variety
Of small mobile creatures
Such as birds, butterflies and crawling insects
To intertraffic and cross-pollinate
The vast variety of vegetation
Sumtotally involved
In the biochemical refertilization complexities
Of ecology.
For instance the honey bees
Buzz-enter the flowers one by one
To reach their honey
While bumblingly knocking off and accumulating pollen
On their bumbly tails
With which entirely inadvertently

To cross-fertilize the next plants
Whose blossoms they enter.

Each biological species
Is technologically designed
To be structurally programmed
By the DNA-RNA coding
While being behaviorally programmed
By its chromosomes
To go directly at 180 degrees
To self-rewarding (feedback) targets
While inadvertently, or unknowingly producing
The cross-fertilizing 90-degree "side effects."
These inadvertent, secondarily rated side effects
Of each of the species' individuals
Serve, sumtotally, to produce
The main recirculatory system
Of terrestrial ecology
Which in turn
Is only a local Universe recirculatory system
Within the comprehensive
Scenario system
Of non-unitarily conceptual
UNIVERSE
Whose prime function is
Eternal self regeneration.

Each special case biological species'
Seemingly "selfish," self-serving,
Inadvertently sustains
The synergetic recircuitry
Of terrestrial ecology
And thereby sustains the human regeneration
Which in turn accommodates
The human mind's
Local metaphysical problem solving
And the latter's at first and for long
Only inadvertent support
Of eternal cosmic regeneration.

All the humans,
Like the honey bee,
Are born ignorant,
And are preprogrammed with
(A)  intuition,
(B)  curiosity,
(C)  speculative assuming,
(D)  exploratory testing,
(E)  hunger,
(F)  thirst,
(G)  respiratory and imbibitory drives
       To assimilate chemically intertransformative elements
       In appropriate crystalline, liquid and gaseous increments,
(H)  procreative urge,
(I)  parental protectiveness,
(J)  an urge to demonstrate competence,
(K)  a fragilely spontaneous trust of others, and
(L)  compassion

Humans with their chromosomically programmed
Direct drives to go after food,
Water, air and sex
Inadvertently produce babies
And many other (to them)
Secondary or side effects
Which inadvertent side effects result
In humans doing the right cosmic regeneration tasks
For any and all wrong reasons—
Or sometimes without any reason at all—
Just driven by fear or longing.

The direct drive effects
Are 180-degree linear, line-of-sight, go-after-it effects
Whereas geometrically speaking
The side effects are 90-degree effects.

Pull on a rope
And it contracts in a plane
At 90 degrees to the axis of the purposive pulling.

Push on a jelly mass
And it bulges out tensively
In a plane at 90 degrees to the axis of pushing.
It has become gradually recognized
By human minds
That the inadvertent 90-degree side effects
Are inexorably inherent
In the 180-degree drives.
Humans find that the sum total
Of all their direct drive requirements
Together with their inexorable side effect involvements
Impose an ever multiplying and inescapable
Complex of supportive responsibilities.
For instance, humans have compulsively to provide
For their inadvertently produced babies.

Humans have had to learn
To get what they needed
For themselves and dependents
Doing so partially by direct production
And partially and often indirectly
Through a complex of intertradings.

With farmers tendering foods
And cobblers tendering shoes
The life support bartering
Became increasingly complex
And finally a common medium of exchange
—Money—was evolved,
Whereafter humans became
"Money bees"
Because money was the all-purpose stuff
That got them what they needed and wanted
When they needed it.

And the inadvertent side effects
Of money-honey bee bumbling by humans
Multiplied, proliferated
And progressively complicated
Family, community, state, national,
And finally all planetary life.

Science long ago discovered
A generalized principle
Eternally operative in Universe
Which they named precession.
Precession is the effect
Of bodies in motion
On other bodies in motion.
For instance, the gravitational pull
Of the already-in-motion Sun
Upon the already-in-motion Earth
Acts precessionally to make the Earth
Orbit around the sun
At 90 degrees to the gravitational pull
And so in turn
Does the Earth precess
Its gravitationally restrained Moon
Into an orbit travelling at 90 degrees
To the direct 180-degree gravitational attraction.
So too do the nuclei of all the atoms
Precess their electrons into orbit
And so do all humans
Precess into orbit about them
All those attracted to them.
And all of the regenerative circuitry
Of recycling Universe
Is precessionally accomplished.

Humans were born ignorant
Of both ecology and precession
As well as
Of all the regenerative circuitry of Universe.
It is not surprising therefore
That chromosomically preprogrammed humans
Have until now consciously responded
Only to the 180-degree attractions
While ecological regeneration thrived
On the myriad of 90-degree side-effect inadvertencies.

What may be called
The *inadvertency phase* of humanity
Is an evolutionary phase
Of preconditioned 180-degree reflexing.
Though the inadvertency phase
Has lasted millions of years
It is only a gestatively behavioral phase
That becomes obsolete
As humans' metaphysical mind
Now comes to discover
The preeminence in human affairs
As well as in celestial mechanics
*Of the principle of precession.*
*Firstly* in terrestrial ecology
And *secondly* in cosmic ecology—
Whereafter humans
In a swift overlapping succession of events
Are about to recommit their endeavors
To direct support of ecological and economic recycling
And to orbitally regenerative effects in general,
As precessionally interproduced
By all independently orbiting cosmic systems.

Led by its youth
Humanity is now entering
Its INDIVIDUALLY RESPONSIBLE
THINKING AND DOING PHASE
And will consciously identify *precession* and *synergy*
As their highest priority
Metaphysical tools.

This abrupt 90-degree reorientation of human affairs
Is now beginning to occur.
Humanity will progressively abandon
Its exclusively 180-degree self-preservation drive
And instead
Will directly support all 90-degree
Omni-inclusive
Cosmic integrity regeneration precessionings.

180-degree all-for-one selfish drives
Are energy depleting, ergo, entropic.
90-degree one-for-all precession
Is both syntropic and synergetic—
It produces progressively more with less.
Money making and sense making are mutually exclusive.
Humanity is about to abandon
The terrestrial game of money making
And is about to take on
The regenerative integrities
Of cosmic accountability.

We can now see that "earning a living,"
I.e., proving oneself to be an exception
To the premise
That man is born to be a failure,
I.e., is an inadequate function,
Is "excess baggage,"
Is "redundant,"
Was a myopic rationalization
Of the selfish
Blind-to-side effects,
180-degree "money bee" drive.
Wherein each individual "specialist,"
Each family,
Each corporation,
Each regional state,
Each sovereign nation,
Each multinational ideological bloc
Irrationalized its chromosomic bias
Through the 180-degree "Look out for yourself"
Entropic dissidence and cosmic dissonance.

Ecology is an old science
And the phenomenon described by the word
Is as old as the billions of years presence
Of biological organisms on our planet.
Farmers of the land
Have throughout the ages

Been familiar with the complex
Of natural interregenerative effects
Of organisms and their physical environments.
Farmers did not know of it as ecology.
That is the name given by science.

Despite its educated knowledge to the contrary
Humanity has been operating
On the unrealistically conditioned
Historical fixation
Of a "wide-wide world"
Of "four corners of the Earth,"
Ergo of a flat Earth
Reaching outward literally to infinity
With you and me at the center
As the arbiters of universal
Events and values.
Into that infinity
Humanity assumed it could shunt
All its ignorantly "unwanted" wastes
And which infinity it also was assumed
Would go right on providing new resources
To replace those which humanity's
Blind 180-degree "honey-money bee" driving had exhausted.
But suddenly the Earth's sphericity
Has returned the unwanted shuntings
All the way around the Earth
To crash into humanity's backsides,
Causing humanity to look around and see
That: we are indeed on a sphere
And: that's all there is of this and that;
And that's that.

After multimillions of years
Of hard trial-and-error-learned lessons
Within only a third of one century
Western world humanity
Has been maneuvered
By a world cartel of honey-money bees

Into a planetary economics cul-de-sac
Of an exclusively petro-fed metabolism.

As all the while humanity was being lullabyed
Into dreaming its pipeline pipe dreams
Which turned into the nightmares
Of Southeast Asia and Middle East guerrillaing,
The world's monetary medium custodians
Were playing supranational tiddledywinks
With humanity's deposits and equities.
Compromisingly patronizing politicians
Lobbied into law an unwitting social acquiescence
To their semantically obscure ecomonopoly strategy,
Whereby in a decade of 10 percent prime usury
In lending the depositors' funds
To accommodate corporate flight
To supranational sanctuary,
While legally financing that flight
By appended provisos to legislation
Which for a quarter of a century
Shunted the annual billions of dollars of foreign aid
Into contracts with U.S.A. corporations
Whenever these corporations were operating
In any foreign country being "aided."
This one hundred billion dollar subsidy
Of the transplanting
Of originally U.S.A. born and bred corporations
Into foreign lands
Accountingly conveyed
The U.S.A. monetary gold stocks
Into foreign countries
Whereafter the U.S.A. politicians
Cut loose from gold the U.S.A. monetary equity
Thereby depreciating U.S.A. citizens' wealth
To 16 cents on its former dollar of international purchasing
    power
While in the same one third of a century
Swelling the U.S.A. national debt from 36 billion dollars
Paying an annual interest of one billion dollars

To a half a trillion dollar debt
Paying an annual interest to the bankers equity account
Of close to the 36 billion dollars
Which was the size of the total 1933 national debt.

But all this legally operated
Monopolization of all the monetary gold
Inadvertently coincided with the laying claim
To their own national petroleum wealth
By the theretofore naively acquiescent
Monarchs of the oil lands
Who overnight parlayed all the world's monetary gold
Into their personal ownership
By upping the price of the petro-pap of humanity.

This brought about a world economic stalemate
Because the owner-sellers
Of the metabolic diet of humanity
Owned also all the purchasing equity.
Wherefor the world monetary game came to a close
And since it is dead
It can't tell you and me that it's dead
But all humanity will soon
Begin to realize that it is dead,
Ergo: the present hiatus.

Soon a computer advantaged world
May adopt the cosmic
Metabolic accounting system
And real wealth will be discovered
To be just exactly
As previously defined in this present discourse.

Thus the world history's
Greatest economic revolution
Will have occurred in a precessional manner
At 90 degrees to the 180-degree-line-of-sight
Of the leading sovereign nations' assumption
Of a strictly gun-resolved war.

The game called money is about to become extinct.
Advantaged by the computer's capability
To inventory, permutate and reevidence
All relevant metabolic information,
Humanity is about to discover
That whatever it needs to do
And knows how to do
It can always afford to do
And that that in fact is only
And all it can afford to do.

Comprehension of the practicality
Of realizing the truths
Is what humanity needs to acquire.
The truth is that
If it knows its universal resource inventory,
If it knows where the resources are,
If it knows its technology,
If it knows what it needs to do
To take adequate care of all people everywhere,
Humanity needs no money.
It needs physical and metaphysical accounting.
The data is now at hand.

Cosmically speaking
Physics recognizes that
No energy as chemical element matter
Or as electromagnetic radiation
Or as gravity
Can get lost
So the physical content of wealth
Cannot diminish.

After World War One the vast
Metabolic self-regenerative effectiveness of machinery
As driven by inanimate energy sources
Was turned to producing farm machinery
Which today does the farming,

Canning, refrigeration, siloing
And transporting of foods
For all people everywhere.

Humans as "cottonpicking" muscle machines
Were ever less needed on the farms
To produce humanity's foods
And no longer needed to be
Where the food grew
In order to be fed
Before the food rotted.
Food became reliably preserved
And potentially distributable to humans
Anywhere around Earth,
On the Moon
Or outward bound space vehicles.

With this historically unexpected
Preservation and distribution development
90 percent of humanity left the land
And drifted into the cities
Hopefully to earn livings
Or just to yield to evolution's
Uncomprehended dictate.

As previously noted in greater detail
We assume the measure of real wealth
To be the magnitude
Of technologically organized capabilities
Of humanity
To cope with the life support
Of so many humans
For so many forward days
Under reasonably predictable
Life-favoring environmental conditions.

Adopting that definition of wealth
It is seen that after World War One
The industrial revolution

Took over food production in the U.S.A.
And inadvertently divorced humanity
From its ecological intimacy.
Thus the last twentieth century generations
Have lost all direct familiarity with ecology
And now have come to rediscover its existence.
That is what occurred in the 1960's.

And every time humanity makes an experiment
It can only learn more,
Ergo the metaphysical know how component of wealth
Can only increase
And wealth of life support capability
Can only and always does increase.
It cannot be spent.
The fallacial concept of spending
Is part of the obsolete game of money-honey making
Played by exploiting the resources
Exclusively for the advantage of the few
On the ignorantly fallacial basis
That there exists an unalterable and fundamental
Earthian inadequacy of human life support resources.

As a consequence of my own
Experience-gained familiarity
With all the foregoing information
And inspired both by personal circumstances
And by the cosmic integrity
Of the family of thus far science discovered
And experientially confirmed *laws of nature*,
I.e., the family of omni-interaccommodative
And only mathematically stateable
Generalized principles,
I resolved in 1927 to precess,
I.e., to make my own 90-degree reorientation
And thus entered as an average healthy human
Into the *INDIVIDUALLY RESPONSIBLE
THINKING AND DOING PHASE*
Of human evolution on planet Earth.

I first undertook
To think out thoroughly
And to state in writing for myself
What I was trying to do.
I have been reprocessing
That statement
For almost a half century.

# What I Am Trying to Do

In 1959 I was asked by the Marquis Publishing Company to state in one unpunctuated sentence exactly what I am trying to do in life. Advantaged by a third of a century's frequent re-editing of my 1927 text I did so in 100 words. As time passed I kept on rewriting it. In 1962 Norman Cousins published it in Saturday Review at its 200 words stage. Now rewritten many times, it consists of approximately 3000 words in one unpunctuated sentence.

ALWAYS EXCITEDLY ACKNOWLEDGING
The a priori infinite mystery
Implicitly revealed
As that which
Though relevant
Always remains
Undiscovered and unexplained
And is popularly overlooked altogether
In the momentary excitement of preoccupation
Only with that which is discovered
And especially with realizations
Of the new human advantaging significance
Of each great scientific discovery
Wherein for instance
Isaac Newton discovers
The rational *geometrical* rate of change
Characterizing the Interattractiveness
Of any two celestial bodies
While their relative distances apart
Vary only at an *arithmetical* rate
Which interattractiveness itself
Let alone its inversely varying
Second power rate of gain
Is neither manifest nor implied
By any of the constant physical characteristics
Of either of the interattracted celestial bodies
When either is considered only separately
And only in the unique terms
Of one or the other's
Integral dimensions/mass/chemistry
And independent electromagnetic properties

And though Newton's mathematically stated law
Of exponentially differing rates
Of inversely covarying
Mass-distance interattractiveness
Of independent celestial bodies
Was thereafter found by science
To be always unfailingly operative
In all macro or micro cosmic
Constellating
As well as in
The dynamic interpositioning
Of all individually remote bodies
Of all complex movements
Newton's discovered law
Never explains
Why
The interattractiveness
Of the remote-from-one-another bodies
Occurs or exists
Nor does it even suggest
What
The invisible interattractiveness
Is
Though whatever it is
Is so comprehensively embracing in importance
As apparently to guarantee
The eternal integrity
Of omni-complexedly
And everywhere ceaselessly
Intertransforming Scenario Universe
And even though we give that unexplained behavior
The name gravity
The name does not explain the mystery
For gravity
Like all scientifically generalized principles
Is inherently synergetic
And synergy means the unique behaviors manifest
Only by whole systems
Consisting at minimum

Of two independent variables
Whose unique system behaviors
Are entirely unpredicted
By any behaviors or characteristics
Of any of the system's components
When each is considered only separately
Wherefor it is ever experimentally demonstrable
That the unpredicted synergetic behaviors
Of strictly assessed system components
Constitute scientific manifest
Of the a priori mysterious
Cosmic integrity context
Within which major scientific discoveries occur
Which context itself always remains unexplained
By such discoveries as Newton's
Of the first power arithmetical
Vs. the second-power geometrical
Constantly intercovarying
Gravitational interattractiveness
Of separate bodies in Universe

And to the best
Of our experientially derived knowledge
Only humans' *minds* can discover
These nonsubstantial interrelationships
Existing only between
And not of or in
Any of the synergetically behaving system's
Plurality of independently orbiting components

For it is also experientially demonstrable
That in contradistinction to humans' minds
Humans' brains always and only
Inventory differentially
The succession of separate
Definitively sensed-in
Special case inputs and recalls
Characterizing each and every
Separate and terminalled experience

Whose separate special case data
Never contain integral physical clues
Explanatory of the synergetic behaviors
Of the omni-interaccommodative
Mathematically generalized principles
Always demonstrably governing
The complexedly overlapping episodes
Of Scenario Universe's
Nonsimultaneous
Multifrequenced and magnituded
Differentially covarienced
Ever intertransforming
Aberrationally limited complementations
And energetic transactions

And being also acutely aware
Of our own corporeal limitations
Yet ever renewably inspired
By personal rediscoveries
Of the cosmic integrity
Which only intuitively suggests
Imminent discovery of further synergetic potentials
Innate and gestating in Scenario Universe
First hints of which
Are realistically noted and sorted
Only within our subconsciously operative faculties
Which subconscious sortings it seems
Once in a while inadvertently produce
Synergetic relationship insights
News of the arrival of which
Are teleo-intuitively communicated
To our consciousness
Only as spontaneous urges
To look again in certain directions
Or to reconsider certain
Tentative concepts
And aware that those subconscious faculties
May be intuitively programmed
To search consciously

For a reliable and orderly means
Of inducing systematic conceptualizing
Of the significant import to humanity
Implicit in the synergetically gestating events
At the earliest possible system moment
Consciously apprehendable
By truth-coupled human minds
And also assuming that such conceptualizing
Can be directionally oriented
In respect to the environmental geometry
Of self's momentary circumstances
As the conceptualizing relates angularly
To self's head-to-toe observer's axis
And realizing that the dawning sense
Of significant import
Gestating in the subconscious
Which is suddenly emerging
As a discernible generalized principle
Together with spontaneous recall
Of other already proven principles
All of which may be frequency tuned
And discretely quantated
Into special case realizations of now
Thus to serve as a communicable means of entry
Into constructively competent participation by humans
In the strategic decision making
Concerning the special case
Formulative options
To be selectively and successfully realized
And employingly managed
Within the relevant set
Of generalized principles
Governing humanity's
Own evolutionary trending options
While also thereafter permitting humanity's
Responsibly followed-through
Anticipatory design science accomplishments
Of ever more effective and satisfying
Human life support artifacts

Ever increasing those artifacts' functional performances
Per each unit of resource reinvestments
As stated in physical measures
Of work or structure produced
Per each ounce of matter
Each second of time
And each erg of energy therein invested

And employing only
The unique and limited advantages
Inhering exclusively in those individuals
Who all by themselves
Take and maintain the economic initiative
By inventing artifacts
Developing their production prototypes
And proving the latters' capabilities
And safety of use
All conducted responsibly
On behalf of all humanity
As well as on behalf
Of the integrity of Universal regeneration itself
The individual initiatives being always undertaken
In the face of the formidable
Physical capital and credit advantages
Of the massive corporations, foundations
Trade and other special interest unions
And political states
All of whom seek entropically to turn
All such syntropically potential gains
Of Advantage for all
To their own exclusively special advantage

And deliberately avoiding
Political ties and tactics
As well as all negative activities
Social movements and reforms
While also concurrently endeavouring
By experiment, exploration and published data
To inductively excite

All individual Earthians'
Awareness of all humanity's
Syntropically multiplicative potentials
And techno-economically feasible options
As well as humanity's awareness
That only by use of such options
Can humanity effectively cope with
And divest itself
Of its entropically dissipative
Dilemmas and compromises

I *seek*

Through comprehensively anticipatory
Design Science
And its reductions
To physical practices
In the form of inanimate artifacts and services

To participate in nature's multi-optioned
Continuous and inexorable
Reforming of both the physical and metaphysical
Environmental events and circumstances
Instead of trying to reform
Human behaviors and opinions
Which latter is all
That history's political powers
Have ever sought to do

For I am intent
Exclusively through artifact inventions
To accomplish prototyped capabilities
Of providing ever more performance
With ever less resources
Whereby in turn
The wealth augmenting prospects for all humanity
Of such design regenerations
Will induce their spontaneous
And economically successful

Industrial proliferation
By world around
Exclusively *service*-oriented industries
As the regeneratively escalating effectiveness
Of the latters' responsible resource reinvestments
Per each unit of resources reinvested
Render comprehensively obsolete
Any and all economic necessity
To sell buy or own anything
While coincidently obsoleting as well
The economically degenerative practices
Of irresponsible one-way selling-off
Of the world's resources
All of which chain reactions will trend
To ever higher performance attainments
Of the ever improving artifact instrumented services
And thereby will swiftly
Both permit and induce
All humanity
To realize full lasting
Economic and physical success
Plus enjoyment of all Earth
Without one individual interfering with
Or being advantaged
At the expense of any other humans
Now alive or henceforth to be born
And I purpose
Through such responsibly evolving
Performance improvements
Of exclusively service oriented
Artifact instrumented industries
To accomplish universal economic success
Well being and freedom of humans
Together with a sustained abundance
For all foreseeable generations of humans to come
Of all the human life-support essentials
Thereby to eliminate all reason
For further existence
Of any and all varieties of politics

Each of whose ideologies mistakenly say
"We have the best and fairest way
Of dealing with the fundamental inadequacy
Of life support
On our under-resourced
And lethally over-populated
Planet Earth"

And with such design-science-attained
Sustainable abundance for all
Proven to be feasible
And attainable for all humanity by 1985
Will also come obsolescence
Of all the political powers'
Historically demonstrated
Ultimate recourse
To hot official
And cold guerrilla warfaring
And conscripted sacrifice
Of the lives
Of whole generations of youth
Upon the fallacious assumption
That war constitutes
The only means of proving
Which political system
Is the fittest to survive
In the misassumedly
Inherently lethal
Game of life
As we have been taught by history
That it must be played

And with such design science attainable
*Elimination by obsolescence*
Of all that humanity
Has learned by experience to be undesirable
Such as power corruptible
Politics and war
There will also come cessation

Of the history-long missassumed
Necessity for individuals
To *earn* their livings
That is to prove themselves to be
Extraordinarily valuable exceptions to the dictum
That humanity is meant to be a failure

And all the sovereign political states
Will also become obsolete
As will also all economic competition
For any special profit
For any state, corporation or individual
And the world will become preoccupied
With recirculating all its chemical elements
Which as they are totally recycled
At an average rate of every twenty-two years
Will be progressively reinvested
With the ever more effective
Interim gained "know how"
Thus making also obsolete
One-way dead ended wastes
And scrap monger withholdings
To escalate price structures

And the most important obsolescence making
Will be the elimination
Of humanity's most self-destructive weapon
The Lie
For Universe operates only on truth

And it is the most outstanding truth
Of this moment
That we have arrived at the threshold
Of new human functioning in Universe
Which functioning can only be effectively performed
With the prime struggle just to survive
Being completely disposed of
And with it all the debilitative fears
Attendant upon that long struggle

But midway of the threshold crossing
Comes the realization
That the only alternative to that success
Is the self-destruction of humanity

And whether we are to be
A complete success or utter failure
Is in such critical balance
That every smallest
Human test of integrity
Every smallest moment-to-moment decision
Tips the scales affirmatively or negatively
Wherefor we recognize that
It is both fear and ignorance
That delays popular comprehension
Of its historically unprecedented option
Of total human success

For fear secretly grips all wage and salary earners
As well as all political and private bureaucracies
Wherefor I realize that all humanity
Is plunging into an unprecedented state of revolution
Which if proving to be predominantly bloody and physical
Will probably terminate human occupancy of EARTH

Or if, predominantly, metaphysically coped with
As a comprehensive design revolution
Will probably insure the presence of Earthians
For millenniums to come

For the design revolution
To which I am committed
Is the metaphysical and positively objective counterpart
Of Mahatma Gandhi's
Subjectively passive resistance
And if design science wins
Each human henceforth will function
In predominantly metaphysical ways

In our cosmically designed role
As the most effective
Local Universe problem detector and solver
In the spontaneous support
Of the vast complex reciprocal scheme
Of celestial energy's
Increasingly disorderly and expanding
Local entropic stellar exportings
And their elsewhere concomitant
Increasingly orderly and contracting
Syntropic planetary importings
(As for instance here upon planet Earth)
This being the now dawningly realized
Cosmic function of Earthian humans
To solve locally evolving Universe problems
Both physical and metaphysical
Thus locally fortifying the integrity
Of eternally regenerative Universe
Whose cosmic omnicircumferential embracement
Integrates as gravity
Gravity being thereby
Always more vectorally effective
Than the sum of all local and nonsimultaneous
Radial disintegrations of radiation
Even as do a few barrel hoops
Successfully resist
The radially outward escape
Of the individual
Exclusively disintegrative
Crowded together
Individual staves of the barrel
As also myopically preoccupied
Ignorantly disintegrative humans
Are bound together upon our planet
By cosmically embracing benign laws
And necessities of Universe
Such as those guaranteeing the integrity
Of eternally regenerative Universe
Manifest in the invariable relationship

Of cosmically greater effectiveness of gravity
Than the disintegrative effectiveness
Of equally energetically endowed radiation
Which invariable superiority relationship
Is also manifest but ever more comprehensively
In the eternally greater
Cosmic-integrity-guaranteeing effectiveness
Of the always synergetic and syntropic
Metaphysical capabilities
Of comprehensively operative generalized intellect
Over the always energetic and entropic local
Physical capabilities
Which are exclusively operative
Only as local terminal special case episodes
All of which principles succinctly elucidate
The necessitous nature of Universe's grand design strategy
For installing developing and maintaining
The complex problem-solving humans
And evolving their complex ecological support
Upon our local Universe monitoring planet Earth
And it is only
By elimination of all self-deception that the highest
     probability
Of humanity's discovery
Of its metaphysical capabilities can occur
And do so within cosmic evolution's critical time limits
And because it is also true
That only by elimination of all this self-deception
Can this self-discovery be accomplished
Because the a priori otherness
Inherent in the fact of self's birth
And essential to the awareness
Of life itself
Wherefor comes full realization
Of the omni-interdependence
Of all humanity
Which if cultivated instead of frustrated
Will increase synergetically
To provide total physical success of all humanity

Truthful self-discovery being the initial step
Toward humanity's ultimately qualifying
For its unique local-Universe-monitoring functioning
We humans were designedly born
Naked ignorant and helpless
Endowed with the few conscious drives
Of hunger thirst procreation curiosity and fascination
To learn only by ourselves
And only through millions of years
Of often painful trial-and-error experiences
And lonely realizations
That our muscles and physical power
Are utterly subordinate
To our mind's Universe-embracing comprehensions
Wherefor in the trial-and-error struggle for survival
Lasting throughout the past
Millenniums of millenniums
Those exceptional individuals
Who have been fortunate enough
To be able to earn the right to live
Have had to do so
By proving that they had special capabilities
Which seemed functionally essential
To continuance of the successful heirs
Of those fortunate few
Who only by force of superior
Bodily size strength and cunning
Later augmented by arms
Had originally commandeered
The supposedly limited resources
And as yet have the superior weapons
With which to sustain those claims

However the spontaneous
Full life-support franchise
Which has always been accorded
By all humanity
To all new born children

Usually sustained in the past
Until the age of six
Has been progressively extended
In recent decades
First to include primary school years
After which came successively high school
And college years
Then post graduate and doctoral years
For those who wished them

And now with full life support becoming feasible
The scholarship franchise
Will soon become spontaneously extended
By revolutionary necessity
To cover all the living years
Of all humanity

And with life time fellowships for all
Will also come elimination
Of the defensive inferiority complexes
And the historical survival fears
Of all people of all circumstances
Which in the past
Have always frustrated
Humanity's urge to learn for itself
By direct experience and observation
How most effectively to comprehend phenomena
Instead of judging and guessing opinionatedly
As a consequence of credos and dogmas
Relayingly inculcated by others

And with all survival fears of all people eliminated
By universal FULL-LIFE-SPAN Fellowships
To study Universe
And seek understanding
Of the cosmic functions of humanity
Humans will swiftly develop their innate urge
To demonstrate competence
Thus qualifying themselves to participate

In producing services to all humanity
Wherefor the most spontaneous
And popularly sought for privilege of individuals
Will be to qualify for membership
On humanity's research and development teams
Or on its equally significant
Production and service teams
Just as humans now qualify
For participation in amateur athletics
Such activity having become
Completely divorced from
The concept of earning a living

And with the majority of humanity
Engaged in study and self disciplining
Direct experimental discovery
And familiarization with advantages to be gained
By understanding and use
Of the thus far discovered
Generalized scientific principles
Governing all Universe events
Will also come elimination
Of all wasteful daily travel
To the 90 percent of all jobs
Which are the non-wealth-producing
Specialized bureaucratic jobs
Which had been invented
By both private public and governmental
Power administrators
To keep people dependently obligated to them
As well as too busy to make trouble
For the power masters
Whose instincts said
"Divide to conquer
And to keep conquered
Keep divided"
This having always been the prime strategy
Of all the grand strategies
Of all history's power masters

And with such daily travel elimination
Will come vast reductions
In world energy resource consumption

The significance of which
Can be appreciated
When we recall (A) that science has standardized
    the quantifying
Of energy characteristics and behaviors
In terms of lifting a given weight
A given distance outwardly from Earth
In a given quantity of time
As for instance the work done
In lifting one pound one foot in one minute
I.e. in foot-pounds per minute
Or gram-centimeters per second

And (B) that it has also been discovered by geophysics
That each gallon of petroleum
Photosynthesized from Sun radiation
Into hydrocarbon molecules
Regeneratively proliferated by ecological organisms
Harvested and buryingly stored
As concentrated fossil residues
Within this Earth's crust
By wind water and gravitational power investment
Is so long drawn out a process
Requiring so much energy
That it costs nature
*One million U.S.A. 1960 dollars* worth of energy
As combined work pressure and heat
And chemical interexchanging quantities
Stated in scientifically defined constants
Operatively sustained
Over the requisite millenniums of time
Necessary to produce each gallon of petroleum
When that much energy
For that much time
Is priced at the same rate

At which electrical energy is charged to us today
By the public utility companies
Stated on our monthly bills
In money units for each kilowatt hour
Delivered to us of that much energy

Wherefor in Cosmic Costing
Of the regenerative affairs
Of Physical Universe
Wherein all metabolic interexchanging
Is meticulously accounted
To the last unit
Of electron-rest-mass value
Each average automobile commuter
Costs nature several million dollars each day
To go to his ecopolitical-system-invented job
For which work the economic system
Usually pays these right-to-live earners
Far less than one hundred dollars a day
While less than 10 percent of them
Produce any real wealth
Of direct human life support

Which means that a few humans
Who pooled together enough money
To buy enough machinery
To poke pipes deeply in the Earth
Are tapping Universe's progressive
Local energy accumulating
Which when attaining a critical mass magnitude
Some ten billions of years hence probably
Has been designed to inaugurate a new star
To replace others which have burned out

All of which energy accumulating
Cost Universe the one million dollars per each gallon
Which the human needs exploiters
Misassume to have cost nothing
Wherefor they take for themselves

What the money-game calls "pure" profit
Over and above the cost of their mechanical operation
And sell a million dollars cosmic-cost-gallon
For less than one cosmic-cost paper dollar
Which million-for-one is not difficult to do
And dwarfs the historical folly
Of the American Indians
Who sold the Island of Manhattan in New York
To the Europeans
For one bottle of whiskey

And with the popularly proven adequacy
Of life support for all humans
And with Universal recognition
That being born
Makes it mandatory upon world society
That each human is entitled
To healthful growthful lifelong support
Constructive and instructive travel
And access to the full inventory
Of information and knowledge and news
And all of the thus far accumulated wisdom
90 percent of humanity will spontaneously
Disengage from their specious "jobs"
And 90 percent of all the modern
Fireproof business buildings of the world
Will become vacated by the obsolete non-wealth-producing
Exclusively money or political-kudos-making businesses
Permitting those buildings' conversion
Into dwelling studio facilities
Having all contemporary conveniences
Already installed
Most of which conveniences are utterly lacking
Or are only inadequately provided
In the slum flats and squatteries
In which the majority of humanity now dwells

All of which foregoing changes
And their elimination of the survival fears

Exploitation of which always has underlain
All trade union management and political strategies
Will permit technological automation
To produce at 24 hours per day
Rather than for only eight hours
While computer automated travel facility booking
And video-automated matchings
Of all "availables" with all "wanteds"
Will be operative as a 24-hour information services
    continuum
Eliminating all newspapers'
Personal want and merchandise advertising
With vast savings of the newsprint forests
And with satellite sensoring
Of each and all humans' positive and negative
Individual electromagnetic field responses
To given problem solution propositions
Integratively read out
By computerized world monitors
And with world around Satellite relayed telemation
And universal cable TV feedback
And universal two-way TV
Beam and cable feedback
Humanity will come to know instantly
What all humanity's
Reactions and dispositions are
In respect to each and all problems
As they arise
And all humanity will dare to yield spontaneously
To the will of the majority
For if the majority
Makes a wrong judgment
The effect will be swiftly manifest
And the majority can immediately alter the course
Without any negative scapegoating

All of the foregoing and
Its many similar ramifications
When compounded with our now proven capability

To house and service all humanity
At higher standards than
We heretofore have ever experienced
Plus our organized knowledge
Of how to provide all humanity
With an annual energy advantage
Equivalent to the U.S.A.'s of 1972
And do so by 1985
While simultaneously phasing-out
All use of fossil fuels and atomic energy
And deriving our sustainable energy supply
Entirely from our annual energy income
Of Sun power and gravity effects
Ever operative around our planet
As wind water wave tidal
Sun methane alcohol
Eruptive and thermal sources
All of which foregoing
Design science revolution
Will phase out warfare
And release all of humanity's
Highest production technology
From killingry into livingry production
And a world around computerized
Integrated life support system
And with all the foregoing events
Humanity will be reoriented
From its one way entropic
Me-first energy wastings
To its syntropic circulatory
Synergetical you-and-we
Cosmic ecology regenerating functions

All of the foregoing will release
Our minds to perform their unique
Universe searching
Inventing capabilities
And information conserving
In support of which functioning

We humans alone
Amongst all known organisms
Were given conscious intellectual access
To the family of exclusively mathematically stateable
Metaphysical principles
Ever demonstrably governing
The cosmic integrity
Of eternal regeneration
And because the meaning of design
Is that all the parts are interconsiderately arranged
In respect to one another
And because all the generalized principles
Are omni-interaccommodative
Which is to say
That none ever contradict any others
The family of thus far scientifically discovered
Generalized principles constitutes a cosmic design
To which human mind has
The only known access
Other than that
Of the comprehensive
Absolutely mysterious
Intellectual integrity context
Of Universe itself.

# A Definition of Evolution
*Both Physical and Metaphysical*

Environment to each must be
All Universe excepting me.
The Universe in turn must be
All that isn't me plus me.

Physics having found no things,
There are no nouns.
Physics has found only behavioral events
Which can be described verbally
Only by verbs.

Universe is a scenario
Of eternally regenerative events
Comprised of the omni-interactions
Of all the otherness and me.

Metaphysically there is an ever evolving inventory
Of most recently and experientially gained
Weightless information
Within which
Generalized principles are infrequently discerned
Which most recent information inventory
In conjunction with experientially gained
And as yet valid
Earlier information
Ever synergetically alters
Working assumptions
Or improves comprehension
Of the omni-intertransformative nature
Of macro-micro Universe
And modifies the operative criteria

Of conscious existence
Within the ever and everywhere physically transforming
Complementary complexities
Which result in a living
Ever evolving totality of comprehensions
Called Universe, which
Like the dictionary—
     As a total collection of words
     To communicate all the separate
     Nuances of experiences—
Can only be meaningfully considered
One at a time.

Wisdom is the consciousness
Of a confidence, overriding the consciousness
That there coexists a complex,
Comprehensive integrity
Of omni-interaccommodative
Eternally generalized principles
Permeating and embracing
Every demonstrably limited
Special case temporal experience
Which nonsimultaneous complex of phenomena
Ipso facto, can never be
Both individually and simultaneously
Considered and comprehended.
The nonsimultaneity
Can be appreciatively coped with
Only by wisdom,
Which discerns, deliberates and decides
In the terms of the assumed omni-integrity
Of eternally transcendental principles
Known and unknown,
One or more of which unknowns
Are presumably involved
When the confrontations
Are inexplicable
By any as yet discovered generalized principle.

That there is deliberatability is inherent
In the unprecedented synergetic interaction
Of only a few of the principles separated out
From the inventory of totally known principles
Within the as yet discovered—
Yet probably to be increased—
Total complex of eternal principles.
Ergo: from time to time,
Old assumptions prove fallacious
And new unexpected facts of experience confront
Which catalyze the reorganization
Of the total comprehension
Which accrues synergetically as *wisdom*.

Novelty, synergy and the possible presence
Of unknown additional principles
Call for both deliberation
And recognition of the inherent
Fallibility of wisdom itself,
Which fallibility hazard
Wisdom appreciates
As nonwisdom does not.

It is the nature of the history
Of conscious experiences
That information is constantly
Multiplying and changing.
For an instance of the evolutionary processing,

Astrophysics makes it evident
To consciousness
That there are no fixed
Directions of Universe
That can logically be identified
As *up* or *down*.
Consciousness finds
The only reliable directional assumptions
To be *in, out* and *around*
In respect
To various event foci of experience,

Celestial, terrestrial and nuclear,
Wherefore there can be
No further meaningful use
Of the words *up* and *down*.

The metaphysical evolution of wisdom
Is both irreversible and inexorable.
And entropy causes *physical* evolution
Also to be inexorable and irreversible.

The irreversibility and inexorability
Of the entropy
Of all local physical systems' energy diffusions
Can be experientially demonstrated
And mathematically explained
By the variety of interference-occasioned reflections
And refraction anglings
Consequent to energy event interferences
Which are not equal, and alternate
In relative frequency of occurrence
And demonstrate varying nonsynchronous rates
Of energy egress
From any experientially demonstrable
Previous local energy embracements.

What we mean by evolution
Relates strictly
To both metaphysically and physically
Evolving frontiers
Wherein the basic informational assumptions
Of consciousness
Are being progressively altered
Simply or complexedly,
Energetically or synergetically.

Now is the syntropic orderly regrouping,
The only fleetingly identifiable
Evolving consciousness
Of evolving meaning

In respect to the irreversible
Inexorability of change.

Status quo is inherently historical
And is analogous
To the ounces of progressively souring cream
Floating upon the tons
Of milk of experience.
Evolution is a scenario
Of progressive comprehension
By consciousness
And is not predictable
By any single-frame experiences.
Evolution is the scenario
Of eternally regenerative Universe
At its ever more inclusive
And exquisite synergetic eventing.

Status quo
Is a multidimensional tapestry
Of what has been
And will never be again.
And is, ipso facto,
No longer existent.

It is evident
That 99 percent cent of society
Is now preoccupied positively or negatively
Only with status quo,
Ergo, with nonreality,
Ergo, ignorantly.

It is implicit
That the fact of eminent feasibility
Of high standard sustainability of all human life
Now recognized by less than 1 percent of humanity
Must gain a 99-fold amplification
Which involves a 99-fold
Educational reorientation

To synchronize human capabilities
With the inexorable and irreversible
Frontiering of evolution.

This educational regeneration
Is now the highest priority function
Of intellect in Universe.

The only significance and justification
Of human existence in Universe
Is to develop and sustain
The capability of the intellectual functioning
Of ever multiplying wisdom
To cope with the manifold local Universe problems
Attendant upon eternal
Regeneration of Universe.

Hope of humanity's self-validation
Is manifest in the youth of today
Who are casting off
All the conventional educational preoccupations
Which futilely obstruct evolution
And perversely sustain status quo.
Youth is jettisoning
The status quo
As does the chick abandon
Its broken egg shell.

All the king's horses
And all the king's men
Though supported financially
By 200-billion-dollar-a-year
Military budgets—
    And by all the
    World around nonthinking
    Public or private bureaucracies—
Cannot put status quo together again
Nor sustain
Its limited beneficiaries' profitability.

May the great
A priori intellectual integrity
Of eternally regenerative Universe
Grant glorious flight
To the new-born.

# "And It Came to Pass"
## (Not to Stay)

No further time
to ask "War or Peace?"

Planetary revolution is here:
But there are options—
A hot-headedly conducted,
Bloody revolution—
Everyone loses;
A cool-headedly conducted,
Design science computer-accommodated
Wealth-accounting revolution—
All humanity wins.

\*   \*   \*

Amongst the american indians,
it was the *nations*,
not the chiefs or individuals,
who controlled the land.
The Indians assumed that they had
only the hunting, fishing, cultivation and dwelling rights.
All the land, water and sky
belonged exclusively to *The Great Spirit*.
And the same concept was held
By Africans, Eskimos, and Austronesians.
But it was long ago conceded
in Europe and Asia
that whoever owned the productive land
controlled the wealth.
In Europe and Asia
the many individual warlords controlling the lands
were the *owners* of all wealth.
They were the "wealthy."

\* \* \*

How did these disparities of viewpoints and controls occur?

\* \* \*

Many direct questionings of audiences
Of more than a thousand each
Have disclosed that no matter what
Humans think wealth may be
All of the humans questioned felt
That no matter how much wealth they might have
They could not alter one iota of yesterday.

All agreed that whatever wealth may be
It can be articulated
Only now and henceforth.
Wealth is irreversible.

The case of the billionaire on a sinking ship
Who offers to pay a million dollars
For the life preserver
Buoyantly supporting the one and only life belted individual
Floating safely away from the disaster
Which offer the lucky one rejects
Even though finally bid for at the tycoon's limit
Of a billion dollars "cash money"
Proves that money is not wealth
For it cannot buy any "henceforth"
Days of life.

Under omnirealistic conditions
When bluffing and credit are of no avail
Money can be articulated
Neither backwardly, forwardly, nor now.

True wealth *is* the already accomplished
Organization of physical environment resources
By human capabilities
To clothe, shelter, feed,
Protect, inform
And accommodate the initiatives,
And transport requirements
Of human lives.

The magnitude of true wealth consists
Of the number of forward days
Of the number of human beings
Assuredly provided for
By at hand artifacts and consumables.

Including both physical and metaphysical considerations
True wealth consists of: (A) *Energy,* (B) *Know-How.*

A. *Energy* (as intertransformable radiation and matter):
Physics concedes that all the physical evidence discloses
an eternally regenerative Scenario Universe
in which no energy is created
and no energy is lost.
Being cosmically inexhaustible,
the energy content of wealth is constant.

B. *Know-how*
Which can only increase.
All experience always teaches.
We always learn *more*.
The more we learn anew,
the more words we need to communicate
that of which we have newly learned.
The number of words in the dictionary
always increases.
The *Know-how* part of wealth
always increases.
The *Energy* part is constant—
—and cannot decrease.
Therefore, wealth always increases
and all the wealth increase always comes
from increased, experience-born Know-how.
But arbitrary accounting systems
have shunted the *inexorable-wealth growth*,
known as profit,
almost exclusively
into the earning account of the owners
of the physical equipment, premises and raw materials.
Their "balance" sheets show
only the physical assets,
despite the fact that it is only
the metaphysical Know-how
which produces the wealth.
As a consequence,
the present accounting systems
fail to disclose the true state
of terrestrial humanity's wealth

which is now adequate
to support all humanity
and all generations to come
at a higher standard of living
than any humans have ever experienced
or dreamed about.
This is what
only the computer accounting revolution
can clarify for all humanity.
It is the misinformation
emanating from the present inadequate accounting
which may well spark
the hot-headed bloody revolution.

## TRANS-MEANINGS OF WEALTH

Throughout the history of civilizations
people leaders have assumed
the a priori existence
of a fundamental physiological inadequacy
of human life support resources,
which assumed lethal terrestrial inadequacy,
in turn, has given rise
to all major political partisanships
and their respective theories
for resolving which econo-political systems,
and which individuals within those systems,
may be fittest to survive.

Because the cause of this problem seemingly
lay beyond the bounds of *human control,*
it was merciless,
mercy being an exclusively human grace.

But the vast majority of people themselves
remote from and mostly unaware of one another,
were almost entirely illiterate
and quite unaware of their leaders' assumed
planetary inadequacy of life support.
Throughout all past history, people assumed

a sometimes benign, sometimes displeased
divine wisdom to be cosmically operative.

Amongst the less than 1 percent
of humans who had acquired fortunes,
those advantaged by the most secret
technical, economic, and political intelligence
had exclusive knowledge of "the inadequacy,"
and commanded their affairs in such a way
as most probably to sustain their good fortune
by anticipating and exploiting scarcities,
and devoutly proclaimed that
"God helps those who help themselves,"
the evidence for which
as manifest by their own example
seemed undeniable,
ergo, also seemed to fully vindicate
human selfishness,
"certainly" as modestly exercised
in looking out only for one's own dependents.

As, for instance, in a high seas disaster
does each father fight to get his wife and children,
but seldom himself,
into one of the inadequate number
of the ship's undamaged lifeboats.

However, some fathers split-secondly reason
that without their own continuing presence
their families will perish
even though safely reaching land,
and therefore also split-secondly
rationalize it to be
God-given wisdom
that only whole family units
should either be saved or perish together,
ergo, this swiftly rationalizing father
assumes a cosmic obligation
to save himself to save his family.

All the while many a powerful
unmarried male need only
his swiftly remembered
"God helps those etcetera"
to bid him be first
to enter the lifeboat.

From secret time to secret time
in superficially peaceful times
the partisan leader or family head
operating politely,
but enlightenedly
must make a move
which deprives others
of any further chance
of being included
amongst the successfully living.

In "civilized" society
these others-depriving successfuls execute
their too-swift-for-the-eye, rapier-like touches
behind a facade of concerned neighborliness.
Often touché is backhandedly executed
Simply by failure to disclose relevant information
While those they doom
Have no way to know they have been doomed
Until months, or even years, later.

Realistically speaking,
no one has a God-signed deed
to ownership of anything
let alone a cosmically valid deed
to a surveyed plot of land—
all the ground below and the sky above it
as purchased through the "real" estate agency,
and thereby a "legally" acquired title
to a rectangular-sectioned core
of planet Earth

running vertically inward of one's plot
and emerging in the other hemisphere
as one's antipodal acre of land in China,
as well as one's ownership
of the core of sky
reaching outward vertically
through heaven to eternity
through which cosmically-aimed core
stars and asteroids from time to time
trespassingly travel.

What eventually constituted
such "legalized" ownership of land
probably began millions of years ago
when one male human by chance of birth
grew to be much larger than others,
whose size proved of physical advantage
amongst hunting, fishing,
fruit-, nut-, and root-picking people
particularly in tribal survival warring
when the big one said, "that's mine"—
*that* was *that*.

Multi-millennia later
after the lethal demonstration
of the greater range of hitting power
of sling-armed little David
over the bludgeon-clutching giant, Goliath,
the power structure advantage began to shift
from short-armed bulk to distance-armed cunning—
to more with less.

But "legally" documented ownership of land came
only after nomadic berry pickers and hunters,
finding special localities in which grew
the vegetation, fruits, fowl, and animals
most favorable to their life support,
settled and began domesticating
hybrids of such biological growths

which prospered exclusively
within those special geographical environments.

But the *concept* of legal "ownership"
probably originated in an epidemic
of episodes known today
as strong-arm racketeering
which offers "acceptance" of "protection" or *else*.

Coerced "protection" began
millennia ago
when a horse-mounted swordsman
rode up to an unarmed shepherd
tending his flock of sheep in the wilderness
and said, "that's too valuable
a flock of sheep
to be wandering around out here
unprotected by arms
in this dangerous country."

After the shepherd's laughing denial of danger
there came a few nocturnal "or else's"—
many sheep killed or lost—
whereafter geographically-identified *protection* areas
were grudgingly accepted
by the producers of the real life support wealth.

This exercise of lethal power advantage
of the armed over the unarmed—
of the scheming non-wealth-producers
over the innocently preoccupied life support producers—
led to swift overlord claimages
of all the known productively habitable lands
of Asia, Europe, and the Mediterranean world.

Interminable re-takeovers
by the successively stronger
lead, by ever more powerful "mergers and acquisitions,"

to vast sovereign conglomerates
to EMPIRE!

Thereafter major shares
in these, "or else-ings" accomplished,
sovereign realm acquisitions
were *deeded* by the Empire's Emperor
to his prime henchmen
who indeed and by-deed
had shared in the accomplishment of Empire,
the deeds being to vast "Entitled" areas
as Principalities, Dukedoms, and Baronies.

Thereafter these deed-entitled landlords
for further values received
gradually deeded forth to others
ownership of small fractions
of their now socially and financially honored
property titles.

Historically, those who have "owned" the land
have had the best chances of survival:
as provided to the "protector"
by his tenant farmers, herders, huntsmen,
serfs, peons, peasants, slaves, etc.

Ownership of the means of production
identified exclusively as being the land
throughout the long agrarian millennia
has always been accounted
as the prime ingredient
of classical economics' "wealth";
land wealth became identified as capital wealth,
which, as entered onto the ledgers,
gradually included the factory buildings,
and later their fastened-down tools,
their plumbing, wiring, and other fixtures;
legally constituted capital assets
were exclusively physical.

As iron from Minnesota,
manganese from Russia,
and tin from Malaysia
were transported, processed
and combinedly formed into surface-coated
thin sheet metal, non-rusting cans
within which food could be hermetically sealed,
long-lastingly stored and safely shipped
to anywhere around the world
and a myriad of other
only metallurgically realizable
analogous technological events transpired—
including the production and proliferation
of farm-working machinery, motorized transport
and around-the-world split-second
electromagnetic communications networks.
The 90 percent of humanity
that had theretofore worked the farms
in the pre-preservation-of-foods era
and had to live on or near them
in order to be nourished
by the farm produce
ere it or they perish
were suddenly no longer needed on the farms
and no longer needed to live there to survive.
They migrated to the cities looking for jobs.

This whole development concurrently witnessed
the world-around discovery of mining lands.
This was not only a new kind
of capital land wealth,
but a recapitulation of the meaning of wealth
for these mining lands usually existed
elsewhere around planet Earth
than under the farmlands.
Mines were usually located
in geographically remote "colonial" areas
with the ownership of these wilderness mining lands
being claimed by the European land lords

who employed the "credit" of their wealth
to finance the building of the ships,
the voyages of discovery,
the engineer-scientist skills
for working the mines
and the navies to protect
their high seas "lines of supply."
Thus began a new era of capitalism,
that of a world metals cartelism
masterminded by and rigorously ruled by
private international bankers
who extended the credits to the landowners.
This was called finance capitalism.

Then, all unexpectedly, science penetrated
the micro- and macro-ranges of Physical Universe
within whose 99.999 percent invisible reality
the atomics of metallurgy became so comprehended
that all the metals became
both recoverable and recirculatable;
old buildings, machinery,
obsolete armaments and ships
became the new "high-grade" mines.
The total overall tonnage
of old machinery, buildings, and ships
became comprehensively replaced
by more effective and efficient equipment,
in overall twenty-two year regeneration cycles
within which the recirculating metals are progressively
alloyed, formed, and complexedly assembled
in such a manner as to most effectively realize
the enormous interim gains
in scientific and technical "know-how"—
to produce ever higher functional performance capabilities
with ever less investment of energy
as matter, time, and work per function,
while always providing ever more humans
with ever more and ever higher standards
of sustenance and services.

The divorce of the metals
from mine land ownership control
produced two new world wealth controlling groups

    (A) that of the U.S.S.R. and Chinese Communist
        party controls of their successive
        five-year plan industrializations and

    (B) that of the self-perpetuating
        free enterprise, supranational corporation
        managements,
        the latter omni-controlled by a supranational
        know-how-importing-exporting banking fraternity.

Within only this last hundred years
of the astronomically recognized
ten-billion-year history of planet Earth
which is to say within only *one*
*one hundred millionth* of all known time
of Scenario Universe's continuity episodes,
the human conditions on planet Earth
have been so altered
that as we write in January 1976,
52 percent—the majority—of all humanity
is now experiencing a higher standard of living
than ever had been experienced,
or even dreamed of
even by the most powerful royalty,
the richest commoners
and the most privileged of humans
anywhere around Earth
before 1900 A.D.;
a standard of living in which the longevity
of those two billion
advanced way-of-living people
has been approximately doubled,
with nine-tenths of history's diseases conquered,
and their annual miles of normal to-and-froing
increased 50-fold;

a century within which
the time of bodily travel between
the remotest from one another peoples on Earth
has been reduced from 180 days
to one quarter of a day;
World's people have changed from 90 percent illiterate to
     90 percent literate;
and most importantly of all,
a century within which all of humanity
has become intimately and constantly aware
of all one another's presence
around our planet.

Utterly contradicting the validity
of the negative all-history-affecting assumption
of an absolute inadequacy
of terrestrial life support,
it has become experientially demonstrated
that entirely unexpectedly to all history's
working assumptions and predictions,
a new chapter in that history
has suddenly opened, which is led by
    (A) the enormous know-how acceleration
        in doing ever more with ever less
        which can elevate *all* humanity
        to a higher standard of living
        than any have as yet experienced
        and do so exclusively through inanimate artifacts
        which do not oppose, but altogether eliminate
        undesirable customs and functions
        by rendering them obsolete—
        for instance, it long has been recognized
        that "you cannot take it with you—
        (your possessions) into the next world";
        but now we realize that
        "you also cannot take it with you—
        (your possessions) around the world."
        The omni-world-involved progeny
        of today's land (and other immobile property) owners

do not wish to inherit
that which impedes their travel
wherefore *ownership has become progressively onerous.*
The ages-long desirability of property ownership
has been made obsolete
through the implementation of around-the-world living.
This historic termination
of the socioeconomic advantages of immobile property
did not occur as a consequence of a trial-by-arms
    dispossessment
as in all past revolutions.

Now all the landowning syndicates
banks and corporations
are trying to unload their real estate properties
onto individuals through coerced
cooperative and condominium schemes.
The " wise money" is switching its investments
into supranational automated
know-how, service industries.

With the peoples of the world's
one hundred and fifty sovereign nations
utterly unaware of such trending
the world's major socialist party managements
and the supranational banks' managements
who manage the supranational corporations'
integrated regenerative systems
are finding it progressively expedient
to integrate their operations.
Each is discovering the others' strengths
and weaknesses
discovering what may be socialized
and what can only be enterprised.
No matter what systematic methodology
world governance may evolve,
evolution seeks experience-enlightened,
universal, and lasting acknowledgment
of the essentiality of accommodating

pro-social individual initiatives
and the insights of the individual human's mind.
It is essential that all human governance guarantee
the individuals' access to research and development
    resources
adequate to proving the validity
of the individuals' omni-society-benefiting
technological inventions,
as well as to demonstrate the invention's innovative
    advantages
thereby realizable for all humanity.

There is a fundamental difference between the
    commonwealth's
(synergetic) accruals from individuals' initiative
and the exclusively *individual profit* accruals
of such individual endeavors.
The evolutionary integrity of regenerative Universe
requires that the advantages of successful initiative
must always accrue synergetically to commonwealth
thereafter always to be directly reinvested
in further support of individually conceived, served,
realized and proven, more-with-less inventing.
Such discovery and invention initiatings
constitute the headwaters
of the great rivers of know-how
whose flow has now become recognized
as the regenerative essence of wealth augmentation.

We repeat
World revolution is upon us;
Humanity has two options:
    1.  a bloody, pull-the-top-down, political revolution, or
    2.  a bloodless design science revolution
       of exponentially compounding
       20th century science and technology gains
       in accomplishing both ever greater
       and more incisive tasks
       with ever less resources

       per each accomplished function
       for ever more humans.
  (B) which is coupled with
     the now predominantly recirculatory inventory
     of metals and other chemical element-resources
  (C) which in turn is coupled with ecological regenerativity
     and
  (D) is again coupled with the
     eternal cosmic regenerativity of mass-into-radiation-
     and-radiation-into-mass and repeat
     of ever everywhere transforming Scenario Universe
     the realistic accounting of which omni-regenerativity
     makes it altogether incontrovertibly manifest
     that there now exists adequate physical resources
     and metaphysical know-how
     with which, within only one more decade,
     to render all humanity economically successful
     while also accommodating evolutionary growth
     and ever increasing human freedoms,
     as well as providing an equally superior
     physical success for all foreseeable generations.

     Wherefore we now must assume
     *selfishness to be no longer valid,*
     which assumption greatly alters
     not only the validity
     of exclusively private enterprise profits,
     but also the validity of exclusively socialist ideologies,
     within the same cosmic evolution
     which brought about the 20th century's
     utterly unexpected synergetic changes
     transcendentally to all human contriving.

The world-around economies both socialist and private
are trending swiftly to comprehensive service industries
wherein individuals only rent
their homes, vehicles, communication facilities *et al.*,
while corporations only rent

their ever-evoluting machinery and buildings.
This will swiftly induce the development
of vast intercontinental recycling service industries
with computer-time scrapping, stock-piling, renting and
    recovering
of materials and of all chemical elements.
In effect, the world's
metals-bearing public lands
will have been transformed into
a world-governed, world-around metals-renting operation.
*Fixed* properties will have become comprehensively obsolete,
but not as a consequence of political revolution.

And the rented mobile properties
will become progressively
miniaturized and ephemeral.

These great evolutionary trendings
have their unique gestation rates
and cannot be accelerated or retarded

Whereas in 1776
a westward-around-Earth rolling
evolutionary wave deposited
a cross-breeding world peoples
on the North American continent
who declared and effected their independence
from the "or-else protectionism" of the old world
and established themselves
as a democratic federation
of free initiative individuals,
now in 1976, these North American resident
democratically federated, cross-breeding worldians
are declaring their recognition
of the essentiality
of unfettered *interdependence*
of all humanity
the continued frustration of which
by the many fearfully or selfishly biased organizations

may well doom human occupation of our planet.

Concurrently a new era of wealth has dawned
which if not frustrated by selfishness
will eventuate in a world-around acknowledgment,
and be computer accounted as consisting
exclusively of metaphysical know-how
regarding the omnihumanity-supporting capability
of the family of generalized principles
governing the associative and disassociative behaviors
of the gravitationally conserved electromagnetic Universe.

The cosmic hunting and fishing rights will be universal.
The only owner will be the "Great Spirit"—
the nonanthropomorphic god
of the Indians, Eskimos
and all of Earth's earliest
free-ranging humans will be re-cognized.
Mind will have returned
into complete ascendency over matter.

# Soft Revolution

THE EXPONENTIALLY accelerating rate
Of a new world order realization
Is irreversibly emergent
Through chain-reaction emergencies
Transpiring as a primarily invisible
Soft revolution.
As omnihumanity's critical thoughts
Break out as news events,
With the break-outs too swiftly shifting
Their geography
And too frequently multiplying and altering
Their run-off routes
To develop any local power clotures
And consequent burst-out bores
Of sufficient local magnitude
To detonate full-scale hard world revolution,
Yet so far outperforming hard revolutions
In omniegalitarian social advancement—
By elevating the bottom
Instead of depressing the top—
As to be arriving
At a world's socioeconomic ocean
Which levels spherically
To contain any magnitude of local energy outbursts
Such as storms or volcanos
Whose violence is swiftly dissipated
By circumferential wave displacements.

The brimming ocean of commonwealth
Is bound radially by gravity

In a spherical mantle unity
Which when spherically normalized,
Will pulse only
In world tidal integrity
As an omniliterate,
Closed-sphere-system democracy
Consciously, spontaneously, instantly
Rearticulates its wave responses
To world around
Electro-telepathetic info-wave inputs.

The scientifically manifest governability
Of all physical behaviors
Of both macro and micro Universe
By weightless, eternal, omni-interaccommodative,
Mathematically elegant, metaphysical laws
Which in turn are only humanly discoverable
By weightless mind
Suggests that such laws
May also be in governance
Of the operational order of development
Of the universal mind
As born into individual
Local information-processing organisms
Upon planet Earth.

The one common denominator
Of all history's human lives
Which is also exclusively unique
To human experiences
Is their constant confrontment
By weightless, abstract, metaphysical problems
Spoken of as morals, policies, intrinsics,
Aesthetics, mathematical logic, et al.
Which are not involved
In the physiological problems
And chromosomically programmed instructive drives
And subconsciously conditioned reflexes
Of all other biological organisms.

Humans apparently are born
To monitor and prove
The omnidesigning integrity
Of the eternally self-regenerative
Beginningless and endless Scenario Universe
With its vast frequency ranges
Of omni-interpulsative
Yes-no, give-and-take
Radial expansions and circumferential contractions.


Universal mind kaleidoscopically test-resonates
Its anticipatory provisions
For an infinite variety of complementary,
Covariant differentiations of totality—
On one hand into a myriad of omnienvironmental
Evolutionary accommodations of—
On the other hand—local individual organisms
Consisting of a plurality of maximally complex functions
Planetarily situate as biological,
Self-reproducing and regenerating entities;
Some being furnished with integral brain controls,
And one special control group
Wired by the hot line of intuition
To universal mind's front office switchboard,
And with each individual organism
Having its own unique evolutionary life sequences
Of local self realizations
And group attainments
Gradually evolving individually
By trial-and-error discoveries
To final re-emergent synchronization with totality.


Humans have the unique function in Universe
Of coping comprehendingly and objectively
With the subjectively apprehended metaphysical problems
Occurring locally
Whose local solutions are mandatory

To eternally regenerative universe.
Problems, problems, problems!
"The show must go on."
HUMANS ARE ESSENTIAL FUNCTIONS OF
    UNIVERSE.

Mind born into human beings—
Into individuals co-dwelling around planet Earth—
First self-discovers itself
Then "the other"
Mum-mum, M-other.
Then discovers its own physical sensing organism
And begins to remember and to reconsider
The stored and retrieved
Brain coordinate collection of information:
Whereafter it self-discovers
The integrity of its metaphysical mind
And the latter's reaching and penetrating search
To comprehend and deduce
The significant eternal laws potential therein
Which are gleanable only
From out-adequate inventories
Of experience relationships.

In due course the individual mind may comprehend
The cosmically ranging magnificence
Of the transforming totality
Of already mind-harvested knowledge
Thus compounding its unselfish considerations,
And expanding its tolerance
Into appreciative awe
Which altogether synergizes
To generate wisdom.

Wisdom is evolved only by synergy
Which is the behavior of whole aggregates
Not predicted by the separate behaviors of character
Of any one integral part.
Ergo synergy is non-occurrant cerebrally

During monofocus upon self
In preoccupations
Essentially exclusive of others.

The universal mass interattractions called gravity
Of galaxies, star systems and atoms
All manifest *physical synergy*.

And the eternal, mathematical, abstract integrity
Of scientifically generalized weightless principles
Governing all relatively and logical thought
All manifest *metaphysical synergy*.

Love, faith, trust, intuition and wisdom
Manifest *cosmic synergy*
Which is combiningly regenerated
By both metaphysical and physical synergies
Which are inescapably co-joined
With the eternally enveloping and permeating
A priori mysteries
Of whence, why and whither,
Nowhere and nowhen,
The within the withinness
And the without the withoutness.

Due to the myopia of popularized selfishness
Naught is so invisible
As the obvious
Whose immediate relevancy
Can be seen synergetically
Only through deep-focused wide-angled lenses.

Entropy means the initially disorderly
Disengagement behaviors
Of seemingly random energy come-apartness—
Of only locally dying
Individual integral systems
Of the cosmically eternal totality
Of interminable Scenario Universe.

Entropy is the momentary disintegral,
That is, the disintegrative phasing
And expanding disorder
Of relative asymmetry
As viewed relative only
To the disassociating phases
And the abandonments of dying systems
Which phenomena may also be simultaneously witnessed
As syntropic recollections
And increasing orderliness
Relative to new system formulations.

Selfishness is inherently antisynergetic.
Synergy can be socially realized
Only through spontaneous unselfishness.

In due course wisdom discovers
The cosmic evolution pattern
Of its own inexorable growth
To metaphysical mastery
Of physical muscle, brain cunning
And antisynergetically monopolized physical power.

As dominance
Of the metaphysical over physical is accomplished
And of wisdom-born vision
Over short-sightedness
And fear-engendered selfishness—
The perverse affairs
Of progressive self-and-other discovering Earthians
Begin to transform into compatibility
With the omni-integrity of cosmic totality.

But as long as self-consciousness—
Yclept life—continues
The inherent inexactitude
Of Earthian mind's
Self-and-environment apprehending
Will continue only as a dependent function

Infinitely subordinate
To cosmic totality.

But life will—ever and anon—
Experience inspirational glimpsing
Of the orderly cosmic vectors
All of which point convergingly
Toward the absolute truth
Which is incomprehensible
To inherently limited temporality—

Humans were born upon Planet Earth,
Naked, absolutely self-helpless, absolutely ignorant,
But equipped with brain-monitored sensors
With which to apprehend and store
And retrieve for review
Each special case experience.
Humans are also endowed
With memory-reviewing minds.

Once in very rare moments
Individuals using their minds
Progressively discover
Metaphysical and mathematically equatable
Generalized principles
Which are constantly operative
Amongst the behaviors
Of comprehensive special case experience-aggregates
While being utterly unpredicted by the characteristics
Of any of the individual parts.

Human mind later discovers
That these subjectively apprehended principles
Can be consciously and objectively employed
To give humans ever increasing
Technical advantage capability
To cope successfully
With locally interacting events of life
In such a manner as to conserve

Not only humanity's integrally regenerative physical
    organism
But also its metaphysical faculties
While all the time amplifying
The number of days of life
And reducing both physical and metaphysical restraints,
Thus multiplying the exploratory ranging of humans
Throughout the micro-macrocosm
While also increasing proportionally
The number of humans,
And numbers of regenerations of humans to come,
Each to participate ever more consciously
In local evolutionary events of Scenario Universe.

The invention of an utterly ignorant,
Helpless, naked, multibillion-part,
Energy importing, processing and exporting,
Self-building and -regulating organism,
Consisting primarily of water
And operating at a constant temperature of 98.6° Fahrenheit,
Requires also the co-invention, by Universe,
Of complementary environmental conditions
Which operate spontaneously
To look out for the helpless organism
In the most exquisitely detailed electrochemical manner.
Human mothers do not know how to invent their milk-giving
    breasts,
Nor the air which the child must breathe.
Those environmental support features
Are predesignedly provided.

It is implicit that the beginning
Of human life aboard planet Earth
Must have been situate within a complex
Of optimum environmental conditions
Where it could not be killed by:
Freezing, dehydration, slow solar incineration,
Fast volcanic incineration,
Or being eaten by animals
While always remaining adequately moist, cleansed and fed.

These optimum planetary conditions
Are found comprehensively
Only along the palm-shaded,
Shoal-watered, sandy beaches
Inside the barrier coral reefs
Of lagooned islands in mid-tropical ocean waters
Where coconut milk, fish, and fruits abound
And there are no man-eating animals.

Because Vitamin D is essential
To the production of human bone structure
And Vitamin D is only acquirable
From Sun
Through photosynthetic processes of human skin,
And because oversupply of Vitamin D can become lethal,
Nature introduced yellow (carotin)
And dark brown (melanin)
Optical filters into the human skin
Of those most powerfully exposed to Sun radiation.
Where undersupply of Sun radiation occurred,
All color filters were removed
Producing white skin.
Eskimos, having sunlight deficiency,
Receive their Vitamin D from whale blubber,
The only food known to contain Vitamin D.

The earliest humans' skin
Became darkly Sun pigmented.
Successive generations of successful survivors
Had progressively darker skins
Inbred genetically by gene concentration
Of the mutating survivors
Best adapted to environment.

Dwelling for years at the often overwhelming
Mid-ocean interface of sea, land and sky
Human mind discovered the principles
Of floatability, paddle-ability, wind-propell-ability,
Steerability and off-shore navigation.

These extracorporeal mechanisms and knowledge
Permitted humans to explore vast areas
Unreachable by walking or swimming
With man's corporeally integral equipment.

In due course humans reached mainlands,
And, mooring offshore at night,
By day coped with and domesticated
Mainland animals, large and small.

Wearing animal skins on their backs
And on their large hats/huts
They followed their grass-seeking herds
And penetrated the cold uplands.
Intuitively following the life-giving Sun
They deployed northwestwardly
Upon the vastly unfolding Eurasian continent.
Thus humans disappeared
Fanning out geographically
In myriads of separate tribes
Ever more isolated from
And eventually forgotten by one another.
Forced by high mortality
Chieftains often inbred with granddaughters and nieces
Genetically concentrating organic features
Though knowing ought of genetics.
Thus evolved physically differentiated
Separate "nations"
Which are tribes
And not places.

The further north humans penetrated
The more they hibernated
And the more bleached became
Their unexposed skins and hair.

Receiving approximately no Sun,
The palms of all human hands and feet
Are depigmented.

A dark skinned human race originally
Occupied Earth, millions of years
Before their white skinned
Northern progeny evolved.
There is no race other than the human race.

Those who look superficially different
Are the consequences only
Of millenniums of isolation, attrition
And inbreeding of the survival types
Under unique environmental conditions.

So powerful are the climatic pigmentation effects
Of the tropic to arctic
And sea-level to mountain top
Sun-radiation angling
Temperature and humidity differentialings
That the coloring
Of the world's hardwood trees
Ranges from northerly mountainside
White and pink woods
Through torrid zone yellows and reds
To tropical teak greys
And dark brown mahoganies
To equatorial jungle ebony blacks.

These fundamentally dominant inbreeding effects
Are not contradicted
By exceptional cross-breeding cases
Amongst humans and trees
Produced botanically by world around seed blowing
And anthropologically by the vast waterborne shuttling o
    sailors.

If, in fact, there were different races
No political contriving
Could close the psychological gap.

But in fact
There is only one:
The human race.

Unhampered by clothing
The dark skinned worldians of pre-history
Developed greater stature
And physical strength
Than their bewrapped and bleached out
Cold climate cousins
Which paradoxically brought higher prices
For the powerful dark skins
In the slave markets
Into which for millenniums
Asia Minor's war prisoners
Were cashed-in for prize money.

Because the white prisoners' physical inferiority
Provided no market for them
The practice of selling white war prisoners
Had been abandoned
By predominately white Europeans
Before they colonized America
And fought their Revolutionary War
In which white prisoners were not sold;
Thus the true history of the origin of slaves
Was lost to American consideration.
European slave traders purchased
The black prisoners
From the chieftains of victorious
Black African tribes.
They sold them on the American auction block
Exclusively on their physical features.
The black prisoners' unfamiliar languages
Were ignorantly misinterpreted by white settlers
As indicative of mental deficiency.
Ignorant America misassumed
The black skinned people to be
Another and inferior race.

Though man is known to have been present on Earth
For multimillions of years,
We've known with experimental certainty
For only one decade
That undernourishment in the womb
Or during the first year of post-umbilical life
Results in brain damage of human babies.


In order to grow regeneratively
Humans are automated
Through built-in hunger
To take on energy
In the form of food.
Born absolutely ignorant
They were often poisoned
By easy to see, pick and eat
Berries, toadstools and other botanicals.
They learned by observation and experiment
That fresh animals' flesh
Was safe and nourishing.


Large aboriginal men coped with animals
More successfully than did little men,
And thus came to monopolize hunting.
The living animals, conditioned reflexively
By many generations of trial-and-lethal-error
To avoid poisonous vegetation
Had, however, eaten vast quantities and varieties
Of nonpoisonous vegetations and herbs
Thus acquiring a comprehensive diet
Chemically suited for optimum human organism maintenance
Including maintenance of a healthy brain.


Historically the populace in general was forbidden
Under penalty of death
From killing and eating the king's animals.

The proletariat had to make-do
With the weeds, grains, herbs and roots
And their limited chemistries.
Their undernourished babies were born with
Or quickly developed damaged brains.
Bellies filled only with rice
Are chemically undernourished.

The 99 percent comprehensive dullness
Of the impoverished masses of humanity
Has been mistaken historically by both Marxians and kings
As demonstrating the coexistence of two genetic species or
      classes:
1) The clever king stock, and (2) The dull workers.
We now know genetically
That there are neither different races
Nor different classes of humans.

At outset of mainland occupation
Of Earth's dry surface by humans,
Only 1 percent of the land
Was immediately propitious
For sustaining human life.
The propitious locales
Were isolatingly scattered.
Humans, in small, local nations,
Were approximately unaware of each other.
Local kings and their
Only-by-weapons-disputed sovereignties
Were inevitable consequences of the
Geographical isolation—
All of which was a seemingly God-given condition
Both to the 99 percent illiterate humanity
And to the nobles.

That any could be as exceptionally
Fortunate as the king
Was so extraordinary as to render it
Spontaneously logical

That only God could devise such fortune;
Ergo, in all reverence to God
All must reverence the king.

Preindustrial agricultural existence
And its socioeconomic accounting
Was local and seasonal
And limited exclusively
To biologically impounded celestial energy—
"No crops" and the people perished.

In complete contradistinction to farming
Industrialization is universal, evolutionarily continuous
And hooked up directly
To the inexhaustable radiational and gravitational chemical
     energies
Of eternally self-regenerative Universe.

Now a classless raceless humanity around Earth
Is importantly aware of one anothers'
Daily lives and circumstances.

In my lifetime I have witnessed
One and one half billion humans
Attain a higher standard of living
Than that experienced or dreamed of
By any of the kings of my childhood.
This advance of living standard
Has resulted in the doubling
Of their longevity
And a twentyfolding of the area of Earth's surface—
As the stage on which their lives are realized.

The rate of energy mastery gains by humans
In this utterly unpredicted turn of history
Indicates economic success for all humanity
Before 2000 A.D.
If-if-if
In its negative reflexes

Humanity does not blow itself into extinction.
Clearly, evolution is trying
To make all humanity a success
Despite its innate ignorance and millions of years
Of failure and fear-conditioned negativeness.

Increasingly we will see the fearlessly conditioned young
And their innately truthful generation of humanity
Divesting itself of the historically assumed self-misconception
That average man is born to be a failure
And must earn a *living*,
I.e., *prove* his right to live
In order to be considered an exception
And even privileged to participate
In the vitally scarce life-support resources.

Accelerating invisibly
The changing mood of youth
Will throw off all sovereign protectionism
Either local or continental.
A swiftly multiplying *world human*
Will come into majority control
Of social economics
And will have converted the economic accounting system
From an annual profit-and-failure system
To an exclusively successful
Planetary industrial system,
Based on human *life-support* hours produced
As augmented by mind-evolved know-how.
This transition will account
Yesterday's so-called "un-employment"
As constituting historically-won freedom to think
And will be formally supported
By universal research felowships
With which to develop
Humanity's wealth-evolving metaphysical faculties.

This revolution will be accomplished
Unexpectedly, invisibly, emergently
Manifest by a swift set

Of political inadvertencies,
Expediencies, compromises and detente.

Through emergency after emergency will emerge
Utterly unprecedented adjustments
Which will seem so logical to all the world
As to seem quite natural,
Ergo, permitting utter change
Which seems like no change at all.
Thus avoiding all opposition.
This will free automation to start regenerating wealth
At an exponential growth rate
On an around-the-clock,
Around-the-world basis
Employing the already extant
Invisible technology and know-how.

And as humanity comprehensively reconsiders
The myriad nuances of information
There will be synergetically catalyzed
A universal awareness
That humanity is indeed destined
To be as comprehensively successful
As is the hydrogen atom or gravity
And that humanity is now directly geared-in
With the inexhaustible
Physical and metaphysical wealth of the Universe
And can afford not only to do whatever it needs to do—
And right now—
But in fact can afford
Nothing else but success.
Right now!
The alternative is "curtains"
For the little crew of humans
Aboard this approximately inconsequential
Celestial vehicle Earth.
Universe does not put
All of her essential functions
In one celestial basket.

# Ethics

IN THE EVOLUTION of political-economics
Of the late 20th century
There is an emerging pattern
In which yesterday's virtues
Become today's vices
And vice versa
Vices virtues.

We hope this signals the demise
Of either dollar or gun manipulated
Political puppetry's
Overwhelmment of humanity

Throughout the past state
Of innate ignorance of the many.
The informed few
Told the uninformed many
What to do
So that the many's coordinated efforts
Could produce most effectively
The objectives of the few.

And omniwell-informed humanity
Does not need to be told
What needs to be done
Nor how to cooperate synergetically;
It does so spontaneously.

History demonstrates without exception
That successful sovereign power seizers
And successfully self-perpetuating,

Supreme physical power holders in general
Will always attempt to divide the opposition
In order to conquer them
And thereafter keep the conquered divided
To keep them conquered.

Controlling the sources
Of production and distribution
The self-advantaging power systems
Keep the conquered divided
By their uncontestable fiat
That the individual's right to live
Must be earned
To the power structure's satisfaction
By performing one of the ruling system's
Myriad of specialized functions.

The top-gun, self-serving power structure
Also claims outright ownership
Of the lives of all those born
Within their sovereignly claimed
Geographical bounds
And can forfeit their citizens' lives
In their official warfaring,
Which of psychological necessity
Is always waged in terms
Of moral rectitude
While covertly protecting and fostering
Their special self-interests.

To keep the conquered
Controllably disintegrated
And fearfully dependent
"They" also foster perpetuation or increase
Of religious, ethnic, linguistic,
And skin-color differentiations
As obvious conditioned-reflex exploitabilities.

Special-interest sovereignty will always
Attempt to monopolize and control

All strategic information (intelligence),
Thus to keep the divided specializing world
Innocently controlled by its propaganda
And dependent exclusively upon its dictum.

Youth has discovered all this
And is countering with comprehensivity and synergy.
Youth will win overwhelmingly
For truth
Is eternally regenerative
In youth.
Youth's love
Embracingly integrates,
Successfully frustrates
And holds together,
Often unwittingly,
All that hate, fear, and selfishness
Attempt to disintegrate.